101
Quran
Stories
and
Dua

Research and Editorial: Mohammad Khalid Perwez
Art Editor: Mateen Ahmad
Graphic Design: Mohd. Asjad Ali
Illustrator: Gurmeet

First published 2015
© Goodword Books 2015

Goodword Books
A-21, Sector 4, NOIDA-201301, U.P., India
Tel. 91120-4314871, +91-8588822674
email: info@goodwordbooks.com
www.goodwordbooks.com

Goodword Books, Chennai
324, Triplicane High Road,
Triplicane, Chennai-600005
Tel. +9144-4352-4599
Mob. +91-9790853944, 9600105558
email: chennaigoodword@gmail.com

Goodword Books, Hyderabad
2-48/182, Plot No. 182, Street No. 22
Telecom Nagar Colony, Gachi Bawli
Hyderabad-500032
Tel. 04023000131, Mob. 7032641415
email: hyd.goodword@gmail.com

Islamic Vision Ltd.
426-434 Coventry Road,
Small Heath
Birmingham B10 0UG, U.K.
Tel. 121-773-0137
e-mail: info@ipci-iv.co.uk
www.islamicvision.co.uk

IB Publisher Inc.
81 Bloomingdale Rd, Hicksville
NY 11801, USA
Tel. 516-933-1000
Toll Free: 1-888-560-3222
email: info@ibpublisher.com
www.ibpublisher.com

Printed in India

101
Quran
Stories
and
Dua

SANIYASNAIN KHAN

Goodword

Contents

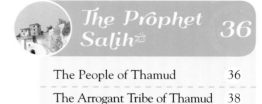

The Prophet Lut ﷺ 58

The Prophet Yusuf ﷺ 62

The Prophet Shuayb ﷺ 88

The Prophets Ayyub ﷺ & Yunus ﷺ 92

The Prophet Musa ﷺ 102

The Prophet Dawud ﷺ 146

The Prophet Sulayman ﷺ 154

The Prophet Isa ﷺ 162

Other Stories 178

The Prophet Muhammad ﷺ 198

The Birth of
Adam﷽ and Hawwa

I am about to create a human being out of clay.

Sad
38:71

Allah said: "Be!" and the entire universe with everything in it came into existence. Allah created Earth, sky, moon, sun, stars, plants, animals, oceans, mountains and rivers. Allah also created angels and jinn. Thus, Allah made the entire universe with all kinds of things in it.

Then, Allah decided to make a human being. Allah collected all kinds of soil and mixed them all like a potter's clay. He

وَتَبَارَكَ ٱلَّذِى لَهُۥ مُلۡكُ ٱلسَّمَٰوَٰتِ وَٱلۡأَرۡضِ وَمَا بَيۡنَهُمَا
وَعِندَهُۥ عِلۡمُ ٱلسَّاعَةِ وَإِلَيۡهِ تُرۡجَعُونَ ﴿٨٥﴾

Blessed be He who rules over the kingdom of the
heavens and the earth and all that lies between
them. He alone has knowledge of Doomsday,
and to Him you shall be returned.

Al-Zukhruf 43:85

8

moulded it into the shape of a man.
Finally, Allah breathed His spirit into it.

Allah named the first man Adam. Then
He created the first woman who was
called Hawwa or Eve. She was the wife of
the Prophet Adam عليه السلام.

Allah loved Adam عليه السلام and Hawwa. Allah
created the universe and the Prophet
Adam عليه السلام out of nothing. Allah has the
power to create anything.

Life in Paradise

"Dwell you and your wife in Paradise and eat freely from it anywhere you may wish."

Al-Baqarah
2:35

Allah asked Adam ﷺ and his wife Hawwa to live in the Paradise. Allah said, "O Adam! Dwell you and your wife in Paradise and eat freely from it anywhere you may wish."

Both Adam and Hawwa lived happily there, eating from the many trees that were provided by Allah for them. Living in paradise was pure bliss. Adam and Hawwa were dear to Allah. Allah loved them a lot. He provided them with all that Adam

رَبَّنَا ٱغْفِرْ لَنَا وَلِإِخْوَٰنِنَا ٱلَّذِينَ سَبَقُونَا بِٱلْإِيمَٰنِ وَلَا تَجْعَلْ فِى قُلُوبِنَا غِلًّا لِّلَّذِينَ ءَامَنُوا۟ رَبَّنَآ إِنَّكَ رَءُوفٌ رَّحِيمٌ ﴿١٠﴾

'Our Lord, forgive us and our brothers who
preceded us in the faith and leave no malice in our
hearts towards those who believe. Lord, You are
indeed compassionate and merciful.'

Al-Hashr 59:10

10

and Hawwa wanted to possess and eat.

But there was one tree which was forbidden for them. Allah told them not to eat from that tree. Allah knew best that it was harmful for them. So He asked them not to approach that tree. The Paradise was a beautiful place for Adam and Hawwa to live in. They lived in the paradise thanking Allah for His favour to them.

The Arrogance of Iblis

'I am better than him. You created me from fire, but You created him from clay.'

Sad
38:76

After creating Adam ﷺ, Allah taught Adam names of all things. Allah had not taught the angels these names, so they did not know any. But Adam knew all, as he was given this knowledge by Allah. Then Allah said to the angels: "Bow to Adam."

All the angels bowed in respect to Adam except Iblis, a Jiin.

بِسۡمِ ٱللَّهِ ٱلرَّحۡمَٰنِ ٱلرَّحِيمِ ﴿١﴾ ٱلۡحَمۡدُ لِلَّهِ رَبِّ ٱلۡعَٰلَمِينَ ﴿٢﴾ ٱلرَّحۡمَٰنِ ٱلرَّحِيمِ ﴿٣﴾ مَٰلِكِ يَوۡمِ ٱلدِّينِ ﴿٤﴾ إِيَّاكَ نَعۡبُدُ وَإِيَّاكَ نَسۡتَعِينُ ﴿٥﴾ ٱهۡدِنَا ٱلصِّرَٰطَ ٱلۡمُسۡتَقِيمَ ﴿٦﴾ صِرَٰطَ ٱلَّذِينَ أَنۡعَمۡتَ عَلَيۡهِمۡ غَيۡرِ ٱلۡمَغۡضُوبِ عَلَيۡهِمۡ وَلَا ٱلضَّآلِّينَ ﴿٧﴾

In the name of Allah, the most gracious the most merciful.
All praise is due to Allah, the Lord of the Universe; the
Beneficent, the Merciful; Lord of the Day of Judgement. You
alone we worship, and to You alone we turn for help. Guide
us to the straight path: the path of those You have blessed;
not of those who have earned Your anger, nor of those who
have gone away from the right path.

Al-Fatihah 1:1-7

Allah asked Iblis, "What prevented you from prostrating when I commanded you to?"

Iblis replied: "I am better than Adam. You made me of fire. But You made Adam of ordinary clay."

Allah said: "Get away from here. I curse you till the Day of Judgment!"

"Give me respite till the Day of Judgment," begged Iblis. He said he would tempt people to sin and lead them away from the right path.

Allah said: "Surely, You shall have no power over my true servants, except those misguided ones will choose to follow you."

The Forbidden Tree

'Go down, all of you, from here.'

Al-Baqarah
2:38

Iblis, Satan and the outcast from the heaven, was not happy at seeing Adam and Hawwa living in the paradise obeying the dictates of Allah. Iblis did not want them to live happily there. So, Iblis deceived them to do against Allah's orders by eating from a forbidden tree.

After eating the fruit from the forbidden tree, Adam ﷺ and Hawwa realised they did not follow Allah's orders. They did not listen to Allah. They ate the fruit from the tree.

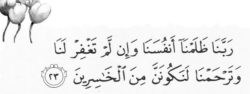

رَبَّنَا ظَلَمْنَا أَنفُسَنَا وَإِن لَّمْ تَغْفِرْ لَنَا
وَتَرْحَمْنَا لَنَكُونَنَّ مِنَ ٱلْخَٰسِرِينَ ﴿٢٣﴾

Our Lord ! we have wronged our souls:
if You do not forgive us and have mercy
on us, we shall be among the lost.

Al-Araf 7:23

They prayed to Allah to forgive them. Allah was very angry. But He loved Adam and Hawwa. He ordered them to leave the Paradise and go down and stay on the earth. Thus Adam and Hawwa started living on earth and from them developed the entire humanity.

The Two Sons of Adam علیه السلام

'God accepts [things] only from the righteous.'

Al-Ma'idah
5:27

The Prophet Adam علیه السلام and his wife Hawwa had two sons. The elder son was called Qabil. The younger son's name was Habil. Qabil was a farmer and Habil was a shepherd. Habil herded sheep, goats and other animals, whereas Qabil worked as a farmer, tilling the fields.

One day they decided to offer a sacrifice to Allah. Habil chose a sheep for Allah. Qabil brought his best crops. Allah accepted the sheep offered by Habil! But Allah did not accept the crops offered by Qabil!

رَبَّنَآ إِنَّكَ مَن تُدْخِلِ ٱلنَّارَ فَقَدْ أَخْزَيْتَهُۥ

وَمَا لِلظَّٰلِمِينَ مِنْ أَنصَارٍ ﴿١٩٢﴾

Our Lord, those whom You condemn to enter
the Fire You have surely brought to disgrace.
Wrongdoers will have no supporters.

Al-'Imran 3:192

16

Qabil was very angry. He began to fight with Habil. He shouted: "I will kill you!" But Habil loved Allah very much. He always had fear of Allah in his heart. He told Qabil to fear Allah. He said calmly to his brother: "Even if you raise your hand to kill me, I will not fight back, for I fear Allah, the Lord of the Worlds."

Qabil was jealous of his brother. He did not listen to him. He began to fight with him and eventually killed him.

Qabil and the Crow

His lower self persuaded him to kill his brother.

Al-Ma'idah
5:30

After killing his brother, Qabil became ashamed of his action. He started to cry. He was full of regret. He did not know what to do with the corps of his brother.

He cried in agony. "Now I have killed my brother, but what shall I do with his body?"

Allah sent a black raven. The raven scratched the ground and showed Qabil how to bury his brother.

رَبَّنَآ ءَامَنَّا فَٱغۡفِرۡ لَنَا وَٱرۡحَمۡنَا وَأَنتَ خَيۡرُ ٱلرَّٰحِمِينَ ﴿١٠٩﴾

Our Lord, we believe, so forgive us
and have mercy on us. You are the
best one to show mercy.

Al-Mu'minun 23:109

"Woe is me!" cried Qabil helplessly. "I am worse even than this raven, for I cannot hide my brother's dead body."

Qabil felt his meanness all the more so, because even a raven could teach him a lesson. When one does things in a rage, it results in humiliation, shame and disgrace. One should not fly into a rage and must fear Allah.

The Peace Loving Brother

If you raise your hand to kill me, I will not raise mine to kill you.

Al-Ma'idah
5:28

Qabil had certainly done a wrong. He had committed a great sin. He killed a person, that too his own brother, without any reason. He had no fear of Allah. Allah was certainly not happy with Qabil.

Allah is happy with those who fear Him. Allah does not like it when we fight and harm others.

قُلْ أَعُوذُ بِرَبِّ ٱلنَّاسِ ۝ مَلِكِ ٱلنَّاسِ ۝ إِلَـٰهِ ٱلنَّاسِ ۝ مِن شَرِّ ٱلْوَسْوَاسِ ٱلْخَنَّاسِ ۝ ٱلَّذِى يُوَسْوِسُ فِى صُدُورِ ٱلنَّاسِ ۝ مِنَ ٱلْجِنَّةِ وَٱلنَّاسِ ۝

I seek shelter in the Lord of people, the King of people, the God of people, from the mischief of every sneaking whisperer, who whispers into the hearts of people, from jinn and men.

Al-Nas 114:1-6

The story of Qabil and his brother Habil teaches us that the two believers should never fight with each other. Even if one of them is bent on fighting, the other one, like the gentle and obedient Habil, should never fight back.

The Prophet Nuh علیه السلام

'O my people, worship Allah; you have no other god but He.

Al-A'raf
7:59

A long time after the Prophet Adam, there was a Prophet of Allah who was sent to the people who had gone astray and did not believe in One Allah. These people did not follow the true path.

The Prophet's name was Nuh علیه السلام. Allah told Nuh to preach to these people. Every day the Prophet Nuh would go from house to house and talk to people about Allah.

He said to his people, "I have come to you with a clear

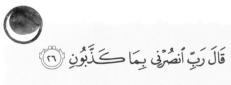

قَالَ رَبِّ انْصُرْنِي بِمَا كَذَّبُونِ ﴿٢٦﴾

Nuh said, 'My Lord, help me! for
they have rejected me,'.

Al-Mu'minun 23:26

warning. That you serve none but Allah. Verily I fear for you the penalty of a Grievous Day."

But the people laughed at the Prophet Nuh ﷷ. They were wicked people. They made fun of the Prophet Nuh ﷷ.

The Prophet Nuh patiently preached to his people for 950 years. But the people still did not listen to him. Only a handful of people accepted his teachings and became true believers. However, majority of them made a mockery of him.

The Great Ark

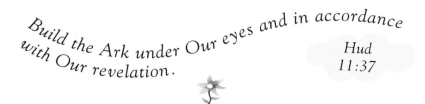

Build the Ark under Our eyes and in accordance with Our revelation.

Hud
11:37

he persistent wickedness of the people of the Prophet Nuh ﷺ displeased Allah. These people did not listen to the teachings of the Prophet Nuh. They continued to make all the mischiefs and did not obey to Allah. Allah was not happy with them. He wanted to punish wicked people. But He wanted to save Nuh ﷺ and the people who listened to him.

وَقَالَ ٱرْكَبُواْ فِيهَا بِسْمِ ٱللَّهِ مَجْرٜىٰهَا
وَمُرْسَىٰهَآ إِنَّ رَبِّى لَغَفُورٌ رَّحِيمٌ ﴿٤١﴾

Nuh said, 'Embark on it. In the name of
Allah, it shall set sail and cast anchor.
Truly, my Lord is forgiving and merciful.'

Hud 11:41

24

So, Allah told Nuh to build a huge Ark.
He ordered him: "build an Ark under
Our watchful eyes."

After a very long period of hard, tiring
work, the Ark was finally ready.

The Great Flood

Embark on it. In the name of God, be its sailing and its anchoring.

Hud
11:41

After the Great Ark was completed, it started to rain heavily. It looked as if the rain was never going to stop! The whole village was getting flooded!

Allah told Nuh ﷺ to embark on the Ark and take with him a pair of each animal species.

Thus the Prophet Nuh along with his believers and a pair of each species boarded on the Ark which moved forward floating on the huge mountain like water waves.

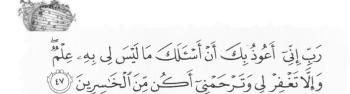

رَّبِّ إِنِّىٓ أَعُوذُ بِكَ أَنۡ أَسۡـَٔلَكَ مَا لَيۡسَ لِى بِهِۦ عِلۡمٌۖ وَإِلَّا تَغۡفِرۡ لِى وَتَرۡحَمۡنِىٓ أَكُن مِّنَ ٱلۡخَٰسِرِينَ ٤٧

'My Lord, I take refuge with You from asking You something of which I have no knowledge. If You do not forgive me and show me mercy, I shall be one of the losers.'

Hud 11:47

The Prophet Nuh's son was among those who had rejected the call of Allah. Nuh called out to his son, "O my son, embark with us and do not be among the deniers." But his son did not listen to him.

Allah was very unhappy with all those who did not believe in the Prophet Nuh. He wanted to drown all people who did not follow the Prophet Nuh. So, all those wicked people were drowned in the flood.

But the Ark was safe for Nuh and his followers and all the animals which were there in pairs.

Mount Judi

The Ark came to rest on Mount Judi.

Hud
11:41

Soon, the flood became even more huge. Water poured down from the sky and the earth burst with gushing spring.

There was water everywhere. No land could be seen. Even the highest mountains were covered with water. The boat with its passengers was carried by the waves. It rolled to and fro and everybody was very afraid. But Allah was watching over them.

Then the rain stopped. The clouds moved away and the sun began to shine. The water started to dry up.

The Prophet Nuh's boat hit Mount Judi and stayed there. Allah

وَقُل رَّبِّ أَنزِلْنِى مُنزَلًا مُّبَارَكًا وَأَنتَ خَيْرُ ٱلْمُنزِلِينَ ﴿٢٩﴾

Say, my Lord, let me land with Your
blessing in a blessed landing place. You
alone can provide the best landings.

Al-Mu'minun 23:29

told Nuh ﷺ to come down. They all left the boat. Happy, they thanked Allah for keeping them safe. In this way, Allah made the flood and the Ark of Nuh a sign and a warning for future generations.

The City of Iram

Who is mightier than we in power.

Fussilat
41:15

L ong ago in the ancient period there was a city called Iram. It was a very big city. The buildings in this city were tall. The gardens were very beautiful. The people were very rich. Iram was the most beautiful city of its time.

The people of this city were known as "the people of the many-columned city of Iram." They made tall buildings with great skill.

رَبَّنَا ٱغۡفِرۡ لِي وَلِوَٰلِدَيَّ وَلِلۡمُؤۡمِنِينَ يَوۡمَ يَقُومُ ٱلۡحِسَابُ ﴿٤١﴾

Our Lord, forgive me, and forgive my parents and all the believers on the Day of Reckoning.

Ibrahim 14:41

But the people of Iram were very proud. They were proud of their city. They were proud of their gardens.

In the beginning they followed the right path. But when they began to prosper, they fell into bad ways and forgot Allah. In their pride, they forgot that Allah gave them everything. They forgot how to pray to Allah.

The Prophet Hud ﷺ

To 'Ad We sent their brother Hud.

Hud
11:50

A Prophet called Hud used to live in this city of Iram. Allah told the Prophet Hud to preach to the people of this city that they should pray to Allah.

The Prophet Hud told them: "Serve Allah, my people; you have no god but Him. You do nothing but fabricate lies."

But the people of Iram did not listen to him. They turned their backs on him. The Prophet Hud knew that Allah did not like arrogant people. He knew that Allah would punish them if they did not change.

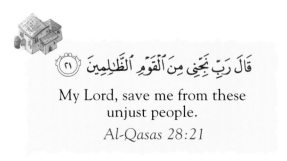

قَالَ رَبِّ نَجِّنِي مِنَ ٱلْقَوْمِ ٱلظَّٰلِمِينَ ﴿٢١﴾

My Lord, save me from these
unjust people.

Al-Qasas 28:21

The Prophet Hud continued to warn the people of Iram: "Do you build monuments on every high place in vanity, and erect castles hoping that you may last forever? When you exercise your power, you act like cruel tyrants. Fear Allah and follow me."

But they would proudly say: "Bring us what you threaten us with?" They rejected the Prophet Hud's call, and called him a foolish man and a liar.

Drought and Wind

So We let loose upon them a raging wind.

Fussilat
41:16

Allah was unhappy with the People of Iram because of their excessive pride and so, Allah wanted to punish these arrogant people . Allah sent a terrible drought. The wells went dry. There was no water in the canals. The leaves dried and fell from the trees.

The Prophet Hud warned the people. He said: "My people seek forgiveness of your Lord and turn to Him in repentance. He will send you from the sky abundant rain upon you."

But the people would not listen. Then Allah sent a terrible wind with dark cloud.

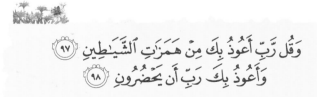

وَقُل رَّبِّ أَعُوذُ بِكَ مِنْ هَمَزَٰتِ ٱلشَّيَٰطِينِ ٩٧ وَأَعُوذُ بِكَ رَبِّ أَن يَحْضُرُونِ ٩٨

Say, my Lord, I seek refuge with You from the prompting of the satans. I seek refuge with You, Lord, lest they should come near me.

Al-Mu'minun 23:97-98

The people thought it was a rain cloud! Their pride made them blind! The terrible wind blew for seven nights and eight days.

The wind smashed their tall and lofty houses. It ruined their garden. The trees fell down with their roots sticking up. The men were dead. There was nothing left of the city! Allah saved only the Prophet Hud and the people who listened to him. Allah always saves those who believe in Him!

The People of Thamud

You built palaces on its plains and carved houses out of the mountains.

Al-A'raf
7:74

A tribe called Thamud used to live in Arabia a long, long time ago. They were great builders. They were greatly skilled in the art of making buildings and castles. They built many towns. Some towns were on the plains. And some towns were in the Rocky Mountains.

They built beautiful palaces and castles in the towns on the plains. Everybody admired them. But they also built towns

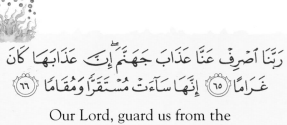

رَبَّنَا أَصْرِفْ عَنَّا عَذَابَ جَهَنَّمَ إِنَّ عَذَابَهَا كَانَ
غَرَامًا ۝ إِنَّهَا سَاءَتْ مُسْتَقَرًّا وَمُقَامًا ۝

Our Lord, guard us from the
punishment of Hell, for its punishment
is most painful to suffer. Indeed, it is
an evil abode and evil dwelling-place.

Al-Furqan 25:65-66

in the Rocky Mountains. These towns were even more beautiful than the towns in the plains. The houses were cut out of the rocks of the mountains. People from far away would come to look at them.

Nobody believed men could make such beautiful houses! But as their material wealth increased, so did their evil ways while their virtue decreased. Tyranny and oppression became prevalent as evil men ruled the land.

The Arrogant Tribe of Thamud

The arrogant leaders said, 'We reject what you believe in.'

Al-A'raf
7:76

The People of Thamud became wicked and mean. They had many wells. But they did not let other people's sheep and camels drink from the wells. They had many green, grassy meadows. But they did not let other people's sheep and camels graze there.

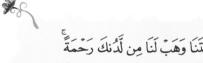

رَبَّنَا لَا تُزِغْ قُلُوبَنَا بَعْدَ إِذْ هَدَيْتَنَا وَهَبْ لَنَا مِن لَّدُنكَ رَحْمَةً إِنَّكَ أَنتَ ٱلْوَهَّابُ ۝ رَبَّنَا إِنَّكَ جَامِعُ ٱلنَّاسِ لِيَوْمٍ لَّا رَيْبَ فِيهِ إِنَّ ٱللَّهَ لَا يُخْلِفُ ٱلْمِيعَادَ ۝

Our Lord, do not let our hearts go astray after You have guided us. Bestow upon us Your mercy. Surely You are a generous Giver. Our Lord, You will surely gather all mankind on the Day of whose coming there is no doubt. God never fails to fulfill His promise.

Al-'Imran 3:8-9

38

Allah sent to the People of Thamud a Prophet whose name was Salih. He was born into the tribe of Thamud. Disappointed to see his people following wrong ways, he asked them to pray the Lord alone.

He said to his people: "Do you think that you will be left secure [forever] -- in the midst of gardens and fountains, and cornfields, and palm-trees laden with fruit -- hewing out houses in the mountains and taking pride in your skill? So fear God and obey me: do not obey the bidding of those who are given to excesses, those who spread corruption in the land instead of putting things right."

But the people of Thamud replied to the Prophet Salih "Surely you are bewitched. You are only a human being like ourselves. Show us a sign, if you are telling the truth."

The She-Camel

My people! This she-camel of God is a sign for you.

Hud
11:64

Allah decided to test the people of Tahmud. Allah sent them a beautiful she-camel. The Prophet Salih told the people to be good to the she-camel. He told them to let the she-camel walk around. He also told them to let her drink cool water and eat fresh grass.

رَبَّنَا لَا تُؤَاخِذْنَا إِن نَّسِينَا أَوْ أَخْطَأْنَا رَبَّنَا وَلَا تَحْمِلْ عَلَيْنَا إِصْرًا كَمَا حَمَلْتَهُۥ عَلَى ٱلَّذِينَ مِن قَبْلِنَا رَبَّنَا وَلَا تُحَمِّلْنَا مَا لَا طَاقَةَ لَنَا بِهِۦ وَٱعْفُ عَنَّا وَٱغْفِرْ لَنَا وَٱرْحَمْنَا أَنتَ مَوْلَىٰنَا فَٱنصُرْنَا عَلَى ٱلْقَوْمِ ٱلْكَٰفِرِينَ ﴿٢٨٦﴾

Our Lord, do not take us to task if we forget or make a mistake! Our Lord, do not place on us a burden like the one You placed on those before us! Our Lord, do not place on us a burden we have not the strength to bear! Pardon us; and forgive us; and have mercy on us. You are our Lord and Sustainer, so help us against those who deny the truth.

Al-Baqarah 2:286

40

But the people of Thamud were mean and wicked. They wounded the she-camel of Allah and then killed her. Not only did they do this but were also mean to the Prophet Salih. They wanted the Prophet Salih to leave their country. They even planned to kill him.

Allah was very angry with them. He made the earth shake and rumble. A terrible earthquake came! It destroyed all their houses. The wicked people died under the ruins. Only the good people were saved.

Allah tests all people. He punishes the bad people. And He helps the good people. He saves them from all danger.

The Prophet Ibrahim علیه السلام

He was a man of truth, and a prophet.

Maryam
19:41

The Prophet Ibrahim علیه السلام was born in a village called Ur in Iraq. He believed in Allah since his childhood. When he grew up, Allah made him a prophet. The people in the Prophet Ibrahim's village did not pray to Allah. They prayed to stones and statues.

One day all the village people went to the market. The Prophet Ibrahim took a hammer and broke the statues one by one, but left the biggest statue with hammer around its neck. When

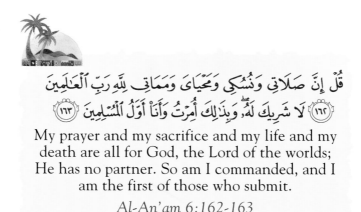

قُلْ إِنَّ صَلَاتِي وَنُسُكِي وَمَحْيَايَ وَمَمَاتِي لِلَّهِ رَبِّ الْعَالَمِينَ

﴿١٦٢﴾ لَا شَرِيكَ لَهُ ۖ وَبِذَٰلِكَ أُمِرْتُ وَأَنَا أَوَّلُ الْمُسْلِمِينَ ﴿١٦٣﴾

My prayer and my sacrifice and my life and my
death are all for God, the Lord of the worlds;
He has no partner. So am I commanded, and I
am the first of those who submit.

Al-An'am 6:162-163

the people came back to the village, they discovered it to their horror. The village people shouted at Ibrahim. They knew that this was his act.

They held him by his hands and legs and threw him into a fire. Allah loved the Prophet Ibrahim a lot. How could Allah let wicked people harm Ibrahim!

Allah said to the fire: "Be cool and a means of safety for Ibrahim!" The fire obeyed Allah and became cool and peaceful. It did not burn the Prophet Ibrahim at all. He was saved!

The Sons of the Prophet Ibrahim عليه السلام

Praise be to God who has bestowed upon me, despite my old age, Ismail and Ishaq.

Ibrahim 14:39

The Prophet Ibrahim did not have any offspring. He travelled from one village to another and told the people about Allah.

He and his wife Sarah once travelled to Haran, and then to Palestine. Then from Palestine he went to Egypt.

In Egypt, the Prophet Ibrahim عليه السلام married an Egyptian lady whose name was Hajar. And from her a son was born who was

رَبِّ ٱجْعَلْنِى مُقِيمَ ٱلصَّلَوٰةِ وَمِن ذُرِّيَّتِى ۚ رَبَّنَا وَتَقَبَّلْ دُعَآءِ
﴿٤٠﴾ رَبَّنَا ٱغْفِرْ لِى وَلِوَٰلِدَىَّ وَلِلْمُؤْمِنِينَ يَوْمَ يَقُومُ ٱلْحِسَابُ ﴿٤١﴾

Lord, grant that I may keep up the prayer, and so may my offspring. My Lord, accept my prayer. Forgive me, Lord, and forgive my parents and all the believers on the Day of Reckoning.

Ibrahim 14:40-41

called Ismail , who later became a Prophet.

One day, angels called on the Prophet Ibrahim and told him that her first wife Sarah will also bear a son. When Sarah came to know she could not believe her ears! For long she had wanted a son. Sarah and Ibrahim had become old. But Allah blessed them with a son at old age. They named their son Ishaq who also became a Prophet.

Thus, Allah blessed the Prophet Ibrahim with two sons: the Prophet Ismail and the Prophet Ishaq.

Allah's Command

When his Lord tested Ibrahim with certain commands and he fulfilled them.

Al-Baqarah
2:124

One day, after the birth of his son Ismail, Allah told the Prophet Ibrahim ﷺ to go to Arabia with his wife Hajar and Ismail. Immediately the Prophet Ibrahim along with his family set off for Arabia. They travelled for many days. They climbed high mountains. They crossed deep valleys. In the end they reached a great desert. After a while they reached a little

رَّبَّنَآ إِنِّىٓ أَسْكَنتُ مِن ذُرِّيَّتِى بِوَادٍ غَيْرِ ذِى زَرْعٍ عِندَ بَيْتِكَ ٱلْمُحَرَّمِ رَبَّنَا لِيُقِيمُوا۟ ٱلصَّلَوٰةَ فَٱجْعَلْ أَفْـِٔدَةً مِّنَ ٱلنَّاسِ تَهْوِىٓ إِلَيْهِمْ وَٱرْزُقْهُم مِّنَ ٱلثَّمَرَٰتِ لَعَلَّهُمْ يَشْكُرُونَ ﴿٣٧﴾

Our Lord! I have settled some of my offspring in an
uncultivable valley near Your Sacred House, Lord,
so that they might establish their prayers. So, make
people's hearts incline towards them and provide them
with fruits so that they may be grateful.

Ibrahim 14:37

valley. The Prophet Ibrahim  and Hajar and little Ismail got down from the camels.

The Prophet Ibrahim said to Hajar: "You stay here. Keep Ismail with you. I have to go back."

His wife protested and said that how she would manage all by herself in this valley. Ismail was only an infant and the valley looked barren without any other human beings present there. But the Prophet Ibrahim turned around and went away saying that this was the order of Allah which he was following. If this is the Will of Allah, so be it, there will be good in this for us, thought Hajar. When the Prophet Ibrahim reached some distance, he turned around and prayed to Allah to keep Hajar and Ismail safe and sound in the valley.

The Miracle of Zamzam

Safa and Marwah are among the symbols set up by God.

Al-Baqarah
2:158

Hajar and Ismail ﷺ were alone in valley where the Prophet Ibrahim had left them. Suddenly, Ismail started to cry. He was thirsty. Hajar put Ismail on the ground and went looking around for water. Hajar looked for water in the valley. She could not find any well. There were no wells in the valley! She ran here and there. There was no water anywhere. Hajar tried again. She ran between the hills of Safa and Marwa. She looked again for water.

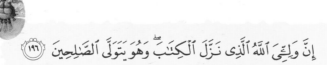

إِنَّ وَلِيِّ ۦَ ٱللَّهُ ٱلَّذِى نَزَّلَ ٱلْكِتَٰبَ ۖ وَهُوَ يَتَوَلَّى ٱلصَّٰلِحِينَ ۝

My protector is Allah who sent down the Book,
for it is He who protects the righteous.
Al-A'raf 7:196

She was very afraid for her son. There was no water anywhere!
She ran back to Ismail. Ismail was lying on the hot sand. He
was crying. He was kicking his legs in the sand. And then there
was a miracle!

There was a hole in the sand near his feet. And there was water
in the hole! It was a spring! Thanks be to Allah! Hajar cried
with joy. She took some water in her hands and gave it to her
son. The spring was later called Zamzam.

The Great Sacrifice

O my son, I have seen in a dream that I am sacrificing you.

Al-Saffat
37:102

One night the Prophet Ibrahim ﷺ was ordered by Allah to sacrifice his son. The next day, the Prophet Ibrahim called Ismail ﷺ. He said: "Ismail, I had a dream last night. Allah wants me to sacrifice you."

Ismail was not afraid. He loved Allah very much. The Prophet Ibrahim and Ismail left Makkah. They went to the valley of Mina. Ismail lay down on the ground.

The prophet Ibrahim stood next to him. He picked up the knife. He was ready to obey Allah by sacrificing his son!

وَإِذْ قَالَ إِبْرَٰهِـۧمُ رَبِّ ٱجْعَلْ هَٰذَا بَلَدًا ءَامِنًا وَٱرْزُقْ
أَهْلَهُۥ مِنَ ٱلثَّمَرَٰتِ مَنْ ءَامَنَ مِنْهُم بِٱللَّهِ وَٱلْيَوْمِ ٱلْأَخِرِ

When Ibrahim said, my Lord, make this city a city
of peace, and provide its inhabitants with fruits,
such of them as believe in Allah and the Last Day.

Al-Baqarah 2:126

50

At this moment the angel Jibril appeared. Allah sent the angel Jibril with a ram to be sacrificed instead.

In this way Ismail was saved. Ibrahim and Ismail thanked Allah. Allah was pleased with the readiness of Ibrahim to sacrifice his beloved son.

Allah was so happy that He commanded the believers to observe this day as Id al- Adha or the Feast of Sacrifice.

The House of Allah

The first House to be built for mankind was the one at Bakkah [Makkah].

Al 'Imran
3:96

One day, Allah ordered the Prophet Ibrahim ﷺ to build the Kabah –the House of Allah –in the valley where Ismail and Hajar were living. The Prophets Ibrahim climbed the hills along with his son Ismail ﷺ. They pushed the heavy stones down and put them in one place. When they had lots of stones, they started to build the House.

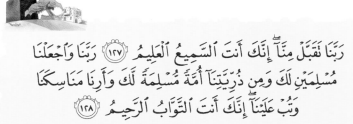

رَبَّنَا تَقَبَّلۡ مِنَّآ إِنَّكَ أَنتَ ٱلسَّمِيعُ ٱلۡعَلِيمُ ﴿١٢٧﴾ رَبَّنَا وَٱجۡعَلۡنَا مُسۡلِمَيۡنِ لَكَ وَمِن ذُرِّيَّتِنَآ أُمَّةً مُّسۡلِمَةً لَّكَ وَأَرِنَا مَنَاسِكَنَا وَتُبۡ عَلَيۡنَآ إِنَّكَ أَنتَ ٱلتَّوَّابُ ٱلرَّحِيمُ ﴿١٢٨﴾

Our Lord, accept this from us; for You are All-Hearing, All-Knowing. Lord, make us bow to You; make of our children and grandchildren a nation that will submit to You. Teach us our rites of worship and turn to us with mercy; You are the Forgiving One and the Merciful.

Al Baqarah 2:127-128

All the time, while building the House of God, they prayed: "Our Lord! Accept this from us. You are All Hearing, All knowing." They also prayed: "Lord, make us submissive to You; make our descendants a nation that will submit to You... our Lord send forth to them a messenger of their own to recite Your revelations to them, to teach them the Scripture and Wisdom, and purify them"

Allah listened to their prayer. Many, many years later, a great prophet was born in Arabia. He was the Prophet Muhammad ﷺ. He was a direct descendant of the Prophet Ibrahim and the Prophet Ismail ﷺ.

The Prophet's Quest

In this way We showed Ibrahim Our kingdom of the heavens and the earth.

Al-An'am
6:75

When the Prophet Ibrahim ﷺ was a young boy, he used to think a lot. Once it was a dark night. The sky was dark. In the darkness, Allah showed the Prophet Ibrahim a star in the sky. It twinkled with a bright light. When the Prophet Ibrahim saw the star, he shouted with joy, 'This is my Lord!' After some time the star went away. The Prophet Ibrahim thought this star could not be my Lord. He said, "I do not love things that set."

رَبَّنَا وَٱبۡعَثۡ فِيهِمۡ رَسُولٗا مِّنۡهُمۡ يَتۡلُواْ عَلَيۡهِمۡ ءَايَٰتِكَ وَيُعَلِّمُهُمُ
ٱلۡكِتَٰبَ وَٱلۡحِكۡمَةَ وَيُزَكِّيهِمۡۚ إِنَّكَ أَنتَ ٱلۡعَزِيزُ ٱلۡحَكِيمُ ﴿١٢٩﴾

Our Lord, send forth to them a messenger of
their own to recite Your revelations to them,
to teach them the Scripture and wisdom, and
purify them. You are the Mighty, the Wise One.

Al-Baqarah 2:129

Then the beautiful moon appeared in the sky. The Prophet Ibrahim again shouted with joy. He said, "This is my Lord!"

The morning light came and the moon went away. The Prophet Ibrahim wondered, "If my Lord does not guide me, I will be one of the misguided people."

In the morning the sun came out. It was shining beautifully. It was shining brightly. The Prophet Ibrahim shouted with joy, "This is my Lord! This is the greatest of all!" In the evening the sun too went away. The Prophet Ibrahim then declared, "My people, I disown all that you worship besides God."

The Prophet Ibrahim looked around. He looked at the trees. He looked at the flowers. He looked at the clouds. A new thought came to the Prophet Ibrahim and he realized that Allah is the Lord of everything. He made the world! He made the sky! He made the sun, and the moon, and the stars!

So the Prophet Ibrahim said, "I have set my face with single-minded devotion, towards Him who has created the heavens and the earth, and I am not one of the polytheists."

The Honoured Guests of the Prophet Ibrahim ﷺ

When they came to him they said, 'Peace!'

Al-Dhariyat
51:25

One day some Angels came to the Prophet Ibrahim in human form. The Prophet Ibrahim did not recognise them. When the angels entered the house of the Prophet Ibrahim, they said, "Peace! Peace!"

After welcoming them, the Prophet Ibrahim rushed inside the house and bought grilled calf for them. He placed it before them. But the angels did not touch the food.

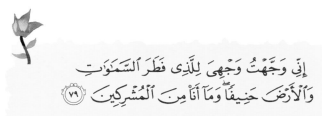

إِنِّي وَجَّهْتُ وَجْهِيَ لِلَّذِي فَطَرَ ٱلسَّمَٰوَٰتِ وَٱلْأَرْضَ حَنِيفًا وَمَآ أَنَا۠ مِنَ ٱلْمُشْرِكِينَ ﴿٧٩﴾

I have set my face with single-minded devotion, towards Him who has created the heavens and the earth, and I am not one of the polytheists.

Al-An'am 6:79

Seeing that the strangers did not touch the food, the Prophet Ibrahim grew afraid of them. But they said, "Have no fear."

Then, the angels gave him good news of a son who would become a wise person. But the Prophet Ibrahim's wife said that she was a barren woman. But the angels said, "This is the will of your Lord. He is the Wise One, the All-Knowing."

Then the angels told the prophet Ibrahim that they have been sent forth to a wicked nation living near the Dead Sea to destroy them because of their sin.

The Prophet Lut ﷺ and the Evil Doers

'How can you commit an abomination such as no one in the world has ever done before you?

Al-A'raf
7:80

Long ago there was a city inhabited by evil doers. The city was located near the Dead Sea. The people of this city were very wicked. They would not listen to good advice. They were totally blinded by the evil inside them. They would waylay, rob and kill travellers.

They also indulged in other demeaning activities. Allah sent to them a prophet. The name of the prophet was Lut. He was

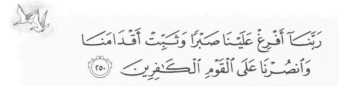

رَبَّنَآ أَفْرِغْ عَلَيْنَا صَبْرًا وَثَبِّتْ أَقْدَامَنَا
وَٱنصُرْنَا عَلَى ٱلْقَوْمِ ٱلْكَٰفِرِينَ ﴿٢٥٠﴾

Our Lord, give us patience, make us stand firm,
and help us against those who deny the truth.

Al-Baqarah 2:250

58

a God fearing man and preached to these people to shun the vices they indulged in. But the people of this city refused to listen. The Prophet Lut warned them of Allah's punishment if they continued doing evil. He told them, "Will you not fear Allah and obey Him? Verily! I am a trustworthy Messenger to you. So fear Allah and obey me".

But the evil people threatened to drive him out of the city. "If you cease not, O Lut, you will surely be banished", they said.

The Terrible Earthquake

When Our command came, We turned that town up side down.

Hud
11:82

The Prophet Lut ﷺ was very sad. The people he was sent to did not listen to him. The people mocked at him and said: "Bring Allah's torment upon us if you are one of the truthful!"

Overwhelmed with despair, Lut ﷺ prayed to Allah to destroy the corrupt men and women. Allah heard his prayer and sent angels to destroy these people.

رَبَّنَآ إِنَّنَآ ءَامَنَّا فَٱغۡفِرۡ لَنَا ذُنُوبَنَا وَقِنَا عَذَابَ
ٱلنَّارِ ﴿١٦﴾ ٱلصَّـٰبِرِينَ وَٱلصَّـٰدِقِينَ وَٱلۡقَـٰنِتِينَ
وَٱلۡمُنفِقِينَ وَٱلۡمُسۡتَغۡفِرِينَ بِٱلۡأَسۡحَارِ ﴿١٧﴾

Our Lord, we believe in You, forgive us our sins and keep us from the punishment of the Fire, those who are steadfast, truthful, obedient, and those who spend [for God's cause] and who pray before dawn for forgiveness.

Al Imran 3:16-17

The angels called on the Prophet Lut and said to him: "Depart with your family while it is yet night and let none of you look back. But your wife will suffer the fate that befalls others."

The night came. Suddenly everything began to shake. The ground shook and it turned upside down. It also began to rain. But it was not raining water! It was hot fire falling from the sky! All the wicked people died, including the Prophet Lut's wife, and nothing was left of the cities.

This is how the angels sent by Allah destroyed the wicked people. Only the good people were saved!

The Prophet Yaqub علیه السلام and The Prophet Yusuf علیه السلام

He will bestow the full measure of His blessings upon you and upon the House of Yaqub.

Yusuf
12:6

Long, long ago in Jerusalem lived a pious old man. His name was Yaqub علیه السلام. He was the grandson of the Prophet Ibrahim علیه السلام and the son of Ishaq علیه السلام, the Prophet Ibrahim's son. Yaqub was himself a prophet, and also the leader of his tribe. The Prophet Yaqub had twelve sons. Yusuf was the Prophet Yaqub's eleventh son and the second child of his first wife. His youngest son was Binyamin, the Prophet Yusuf's own brother.

The Prophet Yusuf's ten older half-brothers had another mother. As a child Yusuf spent his time in and around the

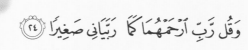

وَقُل رَّبِّ ٱرْحَمْهُمَا كَمَا رَبَّيَانِي صَغِيرًا ﴿٢٤﴾

My Lord, be merciful to them both, as they
raised me up when I was little.

Al-Isra 17:24

family, playing with his little brother Binyamin, running with the baby lambs and gazing out over the vast desert lands.

The Prophet Yusuf had a keen intelligence and a kind nature. His father loved him dearly. He kept Yusuf close to him, and had long talks with him even when Yusuf was still quite young. From the very beginning Yaqub was much impressed by Yusuf. He saw a great and promising future for him.

The Dream of Yusuf ﷺ

Surely, in Yusuf and his brothers there are signs for the inquirers.

Yusuf 12:7

One day Yusuf ﷺ had an unusual dream. In the dream eleven stars and the sun and the moon all bowed down to him. When he woke up, he told his father about this strange dream.

The Prophet Yaqub ﷺ understood right away that his young and best-loved son wold become great one day. This had been made plain in the dream.

رَبِّ قَدْ ءَاتَيْتَنِي مِنَ ٱلْمُلْكِ وَعَلَّمْتَنِي مِن تَأْوِيلِ ٱلْأَحَادِيثِ فَاطِرَ ٱلسَّمَٰوَٰتِ وَٱلْأَرْضِ أَنتَ وَلِيِّ فِي ٱلدُّنْيَا وَٱلْأَخِرَةِ تَوَفَّنِي مُسْلِمًا وَأَلْحِقْنِي بِٱلصَّٰلِحِينَ ﴿١٠١﴾

My Lord, You have given me power and taught me to know the meaning of dreams. Creator of the heavens and the earth, You are my patron in this world and the Hereafter! Make me die in submission to You and admit me among the righteous.

Yusuf 12:101

64

Sensing that his half-brothers might become jealous of him and try to harm him, Yaqub warned Yusuf not to tell them about it: "My little son, do not tell your brothers about your dream lest they hatch a plot against you, for Satan is the open enemy of man."

Yaqub cautioned his son, "The Lord has chosen you, Yusuf, for a higher purpose. He will teach you to interpret dreams, and will perfect His blessings upon you." He told Yusuf that Allah would bless him and their family in just the way He had blessed his grandfather Ishaq and his great grandfather Ibrahim.

The Jealous Brothers

The ten half-brothers were aware of their father's great love for Yusuf ﷺ. They would often grumble saying: "Surely our father is clearly wrong." They were so jealous of Yusuf that they would band together and plot against him. But they did not dare tease him or hurt him openly. The Prophet Yaqub was always nearby and would be very angry.

The young Yusuf was innocent and did not even suspect his brothers' hatred. The ten brothers not only hated their innocent younger half-brothers, Yusuf and Binyamin, but they were disrespectful to their father.

تَبَٰرَكَ ٱسۡمُ رَبِّكَ ذِى ٱلۡجَلَٰلِ وَٱلۡإِكۡرَامِ ٧٨

Blessed be your Lord's name,
full of glory and majesty!
Al-Rahman 55:78

"Surely Yusuf and his brother are dearer to our father than ourselves, although we are a band. Truly, our father is clearly mistaken", they would say to each other.

Yaqub was nothing of the sort. Like his father Ishaq and grandfather Ibrahim, Yaqub was a wise and noble man, a prophet who had been commanded by Allah to pass on the knowledge of the One God to the tribe and to the family.

The Dry Well and the Prophet Yusuf علیه السلام

'Do not kill Yusuf, but if you must do something, cast him into the bottom of a well.'

Yusuf
12:10

One day the ten elder brothers of the Prophet Yusuf asked their father to let Yusuf come out with them and play while they will graze the sheep. The Prophet Yaqub علیه السلام did not like this idea. But he let the Prophet Yusuf go with his elder brothers.

When brothers were a little away from the village, they got hold of the Prophet Yusuf. Then they threw him into a dry

قَالَ إِنَّمَآ أَشْكُواْ بَثِّي وَحُزْنِي إِلَى ٱللَّهِ وَأَعْلَمُ
مِنَ ٱللَّهِ مَا لَا تَعْلَمُونَ ٨٦

He said, I complain of my anguish and my sorrow only to Allah. Allah has made known to me things that you do not know.

Yusuf 12:86

well. The Prophet Yusuf landed at the bottom of the well. He looked up. He could see sky far above his head. The well was very deep. Little Yusuf could not climb that high. He became very scared. He did not know what will happen to him. But Allah was with him.

Allah revealed to him, "You shall [one day] tell them of this deed of theirs, when they do not realize who you are."

At nightfall, the brothers got back home and told their father that Yusuf was devoured by wolf. But his fathers did not believe them. Instead, he said he would keep patience as Allah says it is best to be patient at the time of despair and loss.

The Prophet Yusuf Reaches Egypt

'Lodge him honourably, he may prove of benefit to us, or we may even adopt him as our son.'

Yusuf 12:21

By chance a caravan was passing by the well where little Yusuf was lying. It was very hot. Both men and camels were very thirsty. One man among them spotted the well. So, one of them went to get some water from the well.

He took a bucket on a rope and dropped it into the well. Then he pulled the bucket up. And what did they see? There was a boy clinging to the bucket! They were very surprised! They

يَٰٓأَيَّتُهَا ٱلنَّفْسُ ٱلْمُطْمَئِنَّةُ ﴿٢٧﴾ ٱرْجِعِىٓ إِلَىٰ رَبِّكِ رَاضِيَةً ﴿٢٨﴾ مَّرْضِيَّةً فَٱدْخُلِى فِى عِبَٰدِى ﴿٢٩﴾ وَٱدْخُلِى جَنَّتِى ﴿٣٠﴾

O soul at peace, return to your Lord, well-pleased, well-pleasing. Join My servants. Enter My Paradise.

Al-Fajr 89:27-30

planned to sell him in the market of Egypt. Some rich man will surely buy him, they thought.

So, in Egypt they sold the Prophet Yusuf عَلَيْهِ السَّلَام to a man called Aziz who was a minister in the court of the king of Egypt. This is how the Prophet Yusuf reached Egypt and grew up there.

The Test and the Prison

'God preserve us! This is no human being but a noble angel!'

Yusuf
12:31

The years passed and Yusuf ﷺ grew into a handsome and charming young man. The Aziz treated him with honor. He quickly learned the language and had become almost like an Egyptian. He was truthful and honest, so people asked his advice and respected his opinions.

The wife of Aziz was not a good woman. She had bad intention. But the Prophet Yusuf kept his distance from her. But the Aziz's wife would take no for an answer. She threatened to send him to prison if he continued to reject her advances.

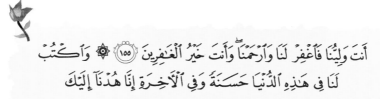

أَنتَ وَلِيُّنَا فَٱغۡفِرۡ لَنَا وَٱرۡحَمۡنَا وَأَنتَ خَيۡرُ ٱلۡغَٰفِرِينَ ۝ وَٱكۡتُبۡ لَنَا فِى هَٰذِهِ ٱلدُّنۡيَا حَسَنَةً وَفِى ٱلۡأٓخِرَةِ إِنَّا هُدۡنَآ إِلَيۡكَ

You are our Protector. Forgive us, therefore, and have mercy on us, for You are the best of those who forgive. Grant us good things, both in this life and in the hereafter. To You alone we turn.

Al-A'raf 7:155-156

Yusuf prayed in great anguish: "O my Lord! I would prefer prison to what these women are inviting me to do. And if You do not avert their guile from me, I may yield to them and so become one of the ignorant."

Even though Yusuf was innocent, later on, they sent him to prison. That was unjust, but it was also Allah's answer to Yusuf's prayer. And, indeed, prison opened up another chapter in the life of the Prophet Yusuf.

The Two Prisoners

'O my Lord! I would prefer prison to what these women are inviting me to do.

Yusuf
12:33

There were two prisoners who entered the prison at the same time as Yusuf ﷺ. Both were servants in the royal court who had displeased the king. One of them was the king's cupbearer. His job was to serve wine to the king. The other was the king's baker. Both were charged with conspiring to poison the king. Both were impressed by the Prophet Yusuf's honesty and wisdom. They trusted him and began to consult him.

إِنِ ٱلۡحُكۡمُ إِلَّا لِلَّهِ أَمَرَ أَلَّا تَعۡبُدُوٓاْ إِلَّآ إِيَّاهُ ذَٰلِكَ ٱلدِّينُ ٱلۡقَيِّمُ وَلَٰكِنَّ أَكۡثَرَ ٱلنَّاسِ لَا يَعۡلَمُونَ ﴿٤٠﴾

All power belongs to God alone, and He orders
you to worship none but Him: this is the true faith,
though most people do not realize it.

Yusuf 12:40.

One night both of them had strange dreams. They came to Yusuf and narrated the dreams. One told him that he saw himself pressing grapes to make wine. The other said that in his dream he saw himself carrying some bread on his head that was pecked at by birds. They requested Yusuf, "to tell us their meaning, for we can see you are a man of virtue." Yusuf replied that they would learn everything before their next meal. He added that his Lord had given this knowledge of interpreting dreams to him. After teaching them the faith, Yusuf interpreted their dreams.

Interprets Their Dreams

'I shall inform you of the interpretation of your dreams before your meal is brought to you.'

Yusuf
12:37

Allah always gives special gifts to His Prophets. He gave the Prophet Yusuf ﷺ a special gift too. He taught Yusuf to understand dreams.

To the prisoner, Yusuf said that he would shortly be released from the prison and would again pour wine for his master. To the other he said that he would be sentenced to death and birds would peck at his head.

Not long after, the Prophet Yusuf's predictions came true. At his trial, the baker was charged with conspiring to poison the king, found guilty, and condemned to death. The charges

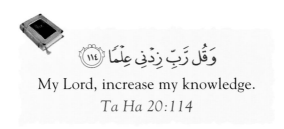

وَقُل رَّبِّ زِدْنِي عِلْمًا ﴿١١٤﴾

My Lord, increase my knowledge.
Ta Ha 20:114

against the cupbearer were proved false; he was released and returned to the palace to his old job.

Yusuf had asked the cup bearer, to relate to the king his own case of cruel and unjust imprisonment. But the cupbearer completely forgot the request, and Yusuf languished in prison for some more years.

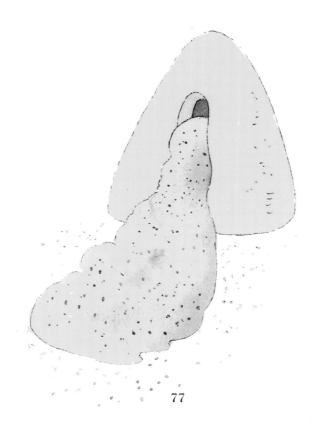

At the King's Court in Egypt

'Bring him to me. I will take him for my special service.'

Yusuf 12:54

In the meantime, one night the king of Egypt had a strange dream. In the dream he saw that there were seven fat cows in a field. Then came seven thin cows and they ate the seven fat cows. After that, the king saw seven green ears of corn. Then these seven green ears of corn turned yellow.

The king was unable to understand this dream. He asked his men to interpret it. But nobody knew the answer.

وَمَآ أُبَرِّئُ نَفْسِى إِنَّ ٱلنَّفْسَ لَأَمَّارَةٌۢ بِٱلسُّوٓءِ إِلَّا مَا رَحِمَ رَبِّى إِنَّ رَبِّى غَفُورٌ رَّحِيمٌ ﴿٥٣﴾

I am not trying to absolve myself: for man's very soul incites him to evil unless my Lord bestows His mercy. Indeed, my Lord is forgiving and merciful.'

Yusuf 12:53

78

Suddenly the cupbearer remembered Yusuf ﷺ and his great ability to interpret dreams. He went to the prophet Yusuf and learnt the meaning of the dream and informed that to the king.

The Prophet Yusuf knew the answer and explained that the dream showed that there would be seven years of good harvest followed by seven years of drought.

The king was very pleased with the Prophet Yusuf. At the King's order the Prophet Yusuf was brought out of prison to the palace before the king.

The king called those who had put him in prison. The innocence of the Prophet Yusuf was clear to the king. He immediately ordered for his release from prison. Then, the king put him in charge of his granaries.

The Brothers and the Cup

'We miss the royal measuring bowl.'

Yusuf
12:72

When the drought came, after seven years of good harvest, the fields became dry. No corn could grow on the dry land. Then the Prophet Yusuf ﷺ opened the granaries. He gave wheat to the people. Nobody went hungry. People from far off areas came to Egypt to collect grains. The brothers of the Prophet Yusuf came too. The Prophet Yusuf recognized them but he did not tell them that he was their brother.
He gave them lots of grain and asked them to come next time with their youngest brother Binyamin.

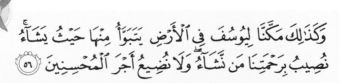

وَكَذَٰلِكَ مَكَّنَّا لِيُوسُفَ فِى ٱلْأَرْضِ يَتَبَوَّأُ مِنْهَا حَيْثُ يَشَآءُ
نُصِيبُ بِرَحْمَتِنَا مَن نَّشَآءُ وَلَا نُضِيعُ أَجْرَ ٱلْمُحْسِنِينَ ٥٦

Thus We caused Yusuf to be established in a
position of authority in the land. He could dwell
therein wherever he pleased. We bestow Our
mercy on whomever We please, and We do not
allow the reward of the righteous to go to waste.

Yusuf 12:56

The following year, the brothers came back to Egypt. This time he had Binyamin with them. On seeing him, the Prophet Yusuf could not control his emotion and took him aside and embraced him, and confided to him that he was his lost brother.

While giving the grains to Binyamin; Yusuf put his cup in his bag. Meanwhile another cup which belonged to the King was lost and everyone's bag was searched. And they found another cup, as expensive as the king's, in Binyamin's bag. As a result, Binyamin was held back. But this reunited Binyamin with the Prophet Yusuf.

The Grief of Yaqub علیه السلام and his Patience

His eyes went white with grief, and he was filled with sorrow.

Yusuf
12:84

When the brothers came back home in Canan, they told their ailing father that Binyamin had committed a theft and that the king's minister had kept him as a punishment. The brothers swore to their father that this was the truth, and they even made the people of the caravan bear witness. Yaqub علیه السلام was absolutely stunned by the story.

اَلَّذِى خَلَقَنِى فَهُوَ يَهْدِينِ ۞ وَٱلَّذِى هُوَ يُطْعِمُنِى وَيَسْقِينِ ۞ وَإِذَا مَرِضْتُ فَهُوَ يَشْفِينِ ۞ وَٱلَّذِى يُمِيتُنِى ثُمَّ يُحْيِينِ ۞ وَٱلَّذِىٓ أَطْمَعُ أَن يَغْفِرَ لِى خَطِيٓـَٔتِى يَوْمَ ٱلدِّينِ ۞

It is He who created me. It is He who guides me; He who gives me food and drink; He who cures me when I am ill; He who will cause me to die and bring me back to life; and He who will, I hope, forgive me my faults on the Day of Judgement.

Al-Shu'ara' 26:78-82

The Prophet Yaqub knew his little Binyamin too well to believe that he had stolen anything. He flatly refused to believe them, thinking they had plotted to get rid of their youngest brother just as they had plotted against Yusuf. So he cried out, "No! Your souls have tempted you to evil. But I will have sweet patience (*sabr jamil*). Allah may bring them all to me... He alone is All-Knowing and Wise."

The loss of Yusuf and now Binyamin was so hard for Yaqub to bear that he lost his eyesight weeping.

"O my sons! Go and enquire about Yusuf and his brother, and never give up hope of Allah's soothing mercy," Yaqub said. "Truly, no one despairs of Allah's soothing mercy, except those who have no faith."

Yusuf ﷺ Forgives his Brothers

No blame [shall fall] on you this day; may God forgive you!'

Yusuf 12:92

So the sons of Yaqub ﷺ once again set out for Egypt in the hope that the king's minister would agree to their request to release Binyamin. Finally they reached Egypt, met Yusuf and pleaded with him to release Binyamin.

They told him that their father was an old man who deeply grieved for his son. They also pleaded with Yusuf for charity as they had not brought much money this time.

قَالَ لَا تَثْرِيبَ عَلَيْكُمُ ٱلْيَوْمَ يَغْفِرُ ٱللَّهُ لَكُمْ ۖ وَهُوَ أَرْحَمُ ٱلرَّٰحِمِينَ ﴿٩٢﴾

He said, 'No blame [shall fall] on you this day; may God forgive you! And He is the Most Merciful of those who show mercy.

Yusuf 12:92

84

To their pleadings, Yusuf replied: "Do you know what you did to Yusuf and his brother?" At once the brothers realized that they were in the presence of Yusuf !

They could not believe their eyes.

"I am Yusuf," Yusuf said, "and this is my brother. Allah has been very generous to us. Those who keep from evil and endure with fortitude will not be denied their reward by Allah."

At first, the brothers feared that Yusuf might want to punish them, but he treated them kindly. They freely confessed their wrongdoing.

But Yusuf was such a kind-hearted person that he did not rebuke them at all. He said, "No blame [shall fall] on you this day; may God forgive you! And He is the Most Merciful of those who show mercy." The brothers were full of amazement, deeply relieved and grateful.

The Family Reunites

He helped his parents to a couch and they all fell down on their knees before him.

Yusuf
12:100

Before the brothers left for home, Yusuf ﷺ gave his shirt to them and told them to touch his father's eyes with it to restore his sight, and to bring his parents to him. As they approached their land, Yaqub sensed that they were near, although they were still some distance from home, because he could smell the scent of Yusuf's shirt.

As soon as the brothers arrived back home, they gave their father the good news that Yusuf was alive and patted his face

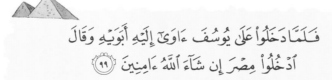

فَلَمَّا دَخَلُواْ عَلَىٰ يُوسُفَ ءَاوَىٰٓ إِلَيْهِ أَبَوَيْهِ وَقَالَ
ٱدْخُلُواْ مِصْرَ إِن شَآءَ ٱللَّهُ ءَامِنِينَ ٩٩

Then, when they presented themselves before
Yusuf, he drew his parents to him and said,
'Welcome to Egypt, in safety, if God wills!'

Yusuf 12:99

with the shirt. Yaqub ﷺ at once regained his sight. He was overjoyed and, thanking Allah, said, "Did I not tell you, Allah has made known to me what you do not know?"

His sons sank their heads in shame and asked for forgiveness. Then, Yaqub's family bade farewell to the land of Canaan. When they reached Egypt, Yusuf embraced his parents and held them in honour. He made them sit on the throne and said: "Welcome to Egypt, in safety, if Allah will!"

Overwhelmed with gratitude to Allah for delivering him from prison, for reuniting him with his parents and for guiding his brothers back to the right path, Yusuf prostrated himself before Allah and thanked Allah for all His blessings.

Madyan and Ayka

O my people, worship God; you have no other god but Him.

Al-A'raf
7:85

adyan and Ayka were two cities on the coast of the Red Sea. They were very important cities in those times. Many ships crossed the sea and came there. In the ships came foreign merchants, who brought beautiful things from other countries to sell in the market.

The people of Madyan and Ayka bought those beautiful things. They loaded them on their camels and they travelled with their

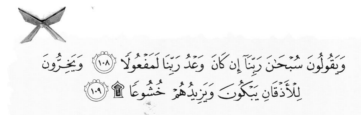

وَيَقُولُونَ سُبْحَٰنَ رَبِّنَآ إِن كَانَ وَعْدُ رَبِّنَا لَمَفْعُولًا ۝ وَيَخِرُّونَ
لِلْأَذْقَانِ يَبْكُونَ وَيَزِيدُهُمْ خُشُوعًا ۝

And say, 'Glory to our Lord! Our Lord's promise is bound to be fulfilled.' They fall down upon their faces weeping, and (the Quran) increases their humility.

Al-Isra' 17:108-109

camels across the desert and sold the beautiful foreign goods to people in other cities.

The People of Madyan and Ayka were very clever traders. They had big shops in the markets. The shops were always crowded. They had many camels to carry their goods to other places.

The Cities Fall Apart

Thereupon an earthquake overtook them and morning found them lying flattened in their homes.

Al-A'raf
7:91

The Prophet Shuayb warned the people of Madyan and Ayka not to give wrong measure and cheat people. He told them that what they were doing was wrong and must reform themselves.

Allah waited for the people to listen to the Prophet Shuayb ﷺ. He waited for them to stop cheating. But the people of Madyan

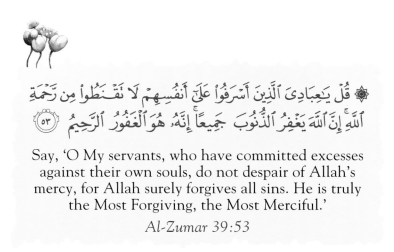

قُلْ يَٰعِبَادِىَ ٱلَّذِينَ أَسْرَفُوا۟ عَلَىٰٓ أَنفُسِهِمْ لَا تَقْنَطُوا۟ مِن رَّحْمَةِ ٱللَّهِ إِنَّ ٱللَّهَ يَغْفِرُ ٱلذُّنُوبَ جَمِيعًا إِنَّهُۥ هُوَ ٱلْغَفُورُ ٱلرَّحِيمُ ٥٣

Say, 'O My servants, who have committed excesses against their own souls, do not despair of Allah's mercy, for Allah surely forgives all sins. He is truly the Most Forgiving, the Most Merciful.'

Al-Zumar 39:53

and Ayka did not bother about what the Prophet Shuayb said. Then a terrible thing happened! Allah sent an earthquake.

The earth trembled. The houses shook, the walls crumbled. Stones from the walls and ceilings fell on the sleeping people. They were crushed to death.

Only the Prophet Shuayb and good people were saved. Allah dislikes cheating. He dislikes lying. He loves people who do not cheat and do not lie. He loves honest and truthful people.

The Prophet Ayyub عليه السلام

A long time ago, in the land of Syria, there lived a prophet whose name was Ayyub علیه السلام or Job. He loved Allah very much. Allah made him wise and rich.

The Prophet Ayyub had many fields. He had many sheep. His house was very big. There were many servants in the house. And his children were very good. The Prophet Ayyub prayed to Allah, thanking Him for the gifts.

The village people said: "It is easy for Ayyub to love Allah. If Ayyub were poor like us, he would never love Allah so much!

فَدَعَا رَبَّهُۥٓ أَنِّى مَغْلُوبٌ فَٱنتَصِرْ ﴿١٠﴾

So he cried out to his Lord, saying,
'I am overcome, so help me!'

Al-Qamar 54:10

He would not pray all the time!" Allah wanted to show people that they were wrong, so Allah put the Prophet Ayyub to the test.

One day, the Prophet Ayyub's sheep got lost. The next day, all the water in the fields and gardens dried up. The Prophet Ayyub became poor. His all family members died except his wife.

The Blessings Restored

We restored to him his family, doubling their number as an act of Our grace.

Al-Anbiya'
21:84

Despite all misfortune, the Prophet Ayyub did not complain. He did not stop praying to Allah.

He knew Allah would help him. He prayed: "I am overcome by distress. But You are the Most Merciful of all those that are merciful." Allah liked the Prophet Ayyub's patience. Allah cured his illness.

وَأَيُّوبَ إِذْ نَادَىٰ رَبَّهُۥ أَنِّى مَسَّنِىَ ٱلضُّرُّ وَأَنتَ أَرْحَمُ ٱلرَّٰحِمِينَ ۞ فَٱسْتَجَبْنَا لَهُۥ فَكَشَفْنَا مَا بِهِۦ مِن ضُرٍّ وَءَاتَيْنَٰهُ أَهْلَهُۥ وَمِثْلَهُم مَّعَهُمْ رَحْمَةً مِّنْ عِندِنَا وَذِكْرَىٰ لِلْعَٰبِدِينَ ۞

Remember Ayyub when he called on his Lord saying, 'I have been made to suffer great distress: but You are the most merciful of the merciful.' We heard his prayer and relieved his suffering, We restored to him his family, doubling their number as an act of Our grace, and as a reminder for the worshippers.

Al-Anbiya 21:83-84

The Prophet Ayyub became well again. Allah again gave him a big house. He gave him fields and sheep. Allah also gave him many children. He made him even richer than before. Because the Prophet Ayyub had showed great patience throughout the worst of disasters, Allah not only rewarded him with great bounty in the Hereafter, but redoubled his former prosperity in this world.

The Prophet Yunus علیه السلام

Remember the man in the whale [Yunus] when he went away in anger.

Al-Anbiya'
21:87

A long, long time ago, in the city of Nineveh there lived a prophet. He was called Yunus, or Jonah علیه السلام.

Allah sends Prophets when He wants to tell people something special. He sent the Prophet Yunus to teach people about Allah.

But the people did not listen to the Prophet Yunus. They laughed at him. The Prophet Yunus got very angry with these

فَسُبْحَٰنَ ٱلَّذِى بِيَدِهِۦ مَلَكُوتُ كُلِّ شَىْءٍ وَإِلَيْهِ تُرْجَعُونَ ٨٣

So glory be to Him who has control over all things. It is to Him that you will all be brought back.

Ya Sin 36:83

people and wanted to go away from the city of Nineveh.

The Prophet Yunus went to the seashore and saw that a ship was about to sail. Without thinking twice, he jumped on and boarded the ship. He wanted to leave the land where people were disobeying Allah.

The Big Fish

And the fish swallowed him while he was blaming himself.

Al-Saffat
37:142

The Prophet Yunus ﷿ boarded the ship which was sailing off the coast. When it reached the middle of the sea, suddenly, it became dark and a strong wind began to blow. A terrible storm tossed the ship to and fro. The sailors and passengers got scared.

The ship was overloaded. They cast lots to determine who would leave the ship. It fell on the Prophet Yunus. The sailors, then, got hold of the Prophet Yunus and threw him overboard.

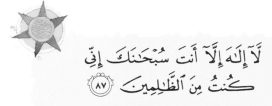

لَّا إِلَٰهَ إِلَّا أَنتَ سُبْحَٰنَكَ إِنِّى كُنتُ مِنَ ٱلظَّٰلِمِينَ ﴿٨٧﴾

There is no deity but You. Glory be to You! I was indeed wrong.

Al-Anbiya' 21:87

The Prophet Yunus tried to swim. But a big fish came and swallowed him. Soon he found himself inside its huge stomach. Frightened, he remembered Allah. He prayed: "There is no god but You! Glory be to You! I have done wrong."

He realised that he shouldn't have run away from his people, as he had not done what Allah wanted him to do!

The Return of Bounty

So We heard his prayer and delivered him from sorrow.

Al-Anbiya'
21:87

Allah heard the Prophet Yunus's prayer. Allah told the fish to take the Prophet Yunus ﷺ to the shore. In no time he found himself on a sandy beach.

The Prophet Yunus rested on the beach. He drank some water from a spring. He ate some juicy fruit from a tree. Then he returned to his home town.

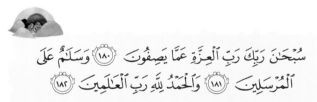

سُبْحَٰنَ رَبِّكَ رَبِّ ٱلْعِزَّةِ عَمَّا يَصِفُونَ ۝ وَسَلَٰمٌ عَلَى ٱلْمُرْسَلِينَ ۝ وَٱلْحَمْدُ لِلَّهِ رَبِّ ٱلْعَٰلَمِينَ ۝

Glory be to your Lord: the Lord of Glory is far above what they say are His virtues. Peace be upon the Messengers and praise be to Allah, the Lord of all the Worlds.

Al-Saffat 37:180-182

The people gathered around the Prophet Yunus. He called them to Allah and warned them of the Day of Judgment. A most surprising thing happened! Everybody began to listen to the Prophet Yunus! Everybody started to pray to Allah!

The Cruel King of Egypt

We showed Pharaoh all Our signs but he rejected them and refused to believe in them.

Ta Ha
20:56

A long, long time ago, a cruel king ruled Egypt. The king was known as Firawn. He did not believe in Allah. And he did not like people who were believers. He hated the Children of Israel. He treated them like slaves.

The Children of Israel had been living in Egypt for a long time. They had settled in Egypt in large numbers since the time of the Prophet Yusuf ﷺ. But Firawn did not like them. One day Firawn told his ministers to kill all the newly born boys of the Children of Israel.

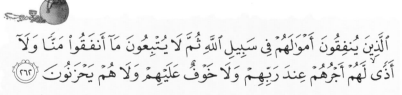

الَّذِينَ يُنفِقُونَ أَمْوَالَهُمْ فِي سَبِيلِ اللَّهِ ثُمَّ لَا يُتْبِعُونَ مَا أَنفَقُوا مَنًّا وَلَا أَذًى لَّهُمْ أَجْرُهُمْ عِندَ رَبِّهِمْ وَلَا خَوْفٌ عَلَيْهِمْ وَلَا هُمْ يَحْزَنُونَ ﴿٢٦٢﴾

Those who spend their wealth for God's cause and do not follow their almsgiving with taunts and insults shall be rewarded by their Lord; they shall have no fear, nor shall they grieve.

Al-Baqarah 2:262

The soldiers of Firawn barged into the houses of the Children of Israel. They searched the rooms and killed all the newly-born boys they found. The king killed these boys without any remorse.

A Chest in the River

Cast him into the river, and have no fear and do not grieve.

Al-Qasas
28:7

In Egypt, there was a little house where lived a man named Imran, his wife Yukabid and their daughter Miriam. They belonged to the Children of Israel.

A little boy had just been born there. They called him Musa, or Moses. They were very afraid that the soldiers might come and find him. Yukabid could not sleep at night. She was scared! She did not know what to do. She prayed to Allah for help.

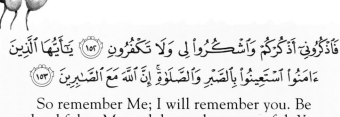

فَٱذْكُرُونِىٓ أَذْكُرْكُمْ وَٱشْكُرُواْ لِى وَلَا تَكْفُرُونِ ۝ يَـٰٓأَيُّهَا ٱلَّذِينَ ءَامَنُواْ ٱسْتَعِينُواْ بِٱلصَّبْرِ وَٱلصَّلَوٰةِ إِنَّ ٱللَّهَ مَعَ ٱلصَّـٰبِرِينَ ۝

So remember Me; I will remember you. Be thankful to Me and do not be ungrateful. You who believe, seek help through patience and prayer; surely, Allah is with the steadfast.

Al-Baqarah 2:152-153

Allah advised her to cast her child in the river and told her not to have any fear as Allah would return her child to her.

Accordingly, Musa's mother put the little Musa in a chest. Then together with Miriam she took the chest to the river. There they put the chest in the water. The waves immediately carried it away.

But the Prophet Musa's mother was very worried. So she told Miriam to walk along the river and see what happened to the baby.

The Kind Queen

'He will be a joy to the eye for me and you! Do not slay him.'

Al-Qasas
28:9

The chest carrying little Musa ﷺ soon was floating by the side of a garden. It was the garden of the queen, the wife of the cruel Firawn. The queen was good and kind-hearted. Suddenly, she saw a chest floating in the river and asked her maid to bring the chest.

When the maid put the chest in front of the queen, she was surprised! There was a beautiful baby sleeping in the chest!

The queen was overjoyed. She said to her husband: "He will be

إِذْ قَالَتْ رَبِّ ٱبْنِ لِى عِندَكَ بَيْتًا فِى ٱلْجَنَّةِ وَنَجِّنِى مِن فِرْعَوْنَ وَعَمَلِهِۦ وَنَجِّنِى مِنَ ٱلْقَوْمِ ٱلظَّـٰلِمِينَ ﴿١١﴾

The Pharaoh's wife said: 'My Lord, build me a house in near to You in Paradise and save me from Pharaoh and his misdeeds. Save me from all evil-doers.'

Al-Tahrim 66:11

a joy to the eye for me and you! Do not slay: he may well be of use to us, or we may adopt him as a son."

And the queen asked her maids to find a nurse for the baby. The Prophet Musa's sister, Miriam, who was watching everything, ran to the queen and told her that she knew a woman who would be a good nurse for the baby. Then, she brought her mother to the queen. Thus, Allah restored Musa to his mother.

Musa ﷺ Leaves Egypt

So Musa departed from the city, fearful and vigilant.

Al-Qasas
28:21

The Prophet Musa ﷺ grew up in the palace of the Firawn. But he knew that his real family belonged to the tribe of the Children of Israel. Musa loved Allah and prayed to Him.

One day Musa was walking in the market. He saw two men fighting. One of them was an Egyptian and other man belonged to the Children of Israel.

Suddenly, the man who belonged to his own tribe called out: "Help me!" Musa ran to help him and hit the Egyptian who suddenly died.

رَبَّنَا ٱغْفِرْ لَنَا ذُنُوبَنَا وَإِسْرَافَنَا فِى أَمْرِنَا وَثَبِّتْ أَقْدَامَنَا
وَٱنصُرْنَا عَلَى ٱلْقَوْمِ ٱلْكَـٰفِرِينَ ﴿١٤٧﴾

Our Lord, forgive us our sins and our excesses. Make our feet firm, and help us against those who deny the truth.

Al 'Imran 3:147

Musa was very upset. He was sorry that he had killed a man. He prayed to Allah: "Forgive me Lord, for I have sinned against my soul." And Allah forgave him.

The next day, however, he found himself in a similar situation. But, all of a sudden, a friend came running to the Prophet Musa and informed him that Firawn's soldiers were looking for him, so he had better run away from the city. The Prophet Musa left immediately and went far away from Egypt.

Musa Helps two Sisters

So Musa watered their flocks for them; and returned into the shade.

Al-Qasas
28:24

After many days of travelling, the Prophet Musa ﷺ reached the land of Madyan. He was tired and thirsty. Soon he found a well. There were also many shepherds around the well with their sheep and cattle. They were watering their flock.

A little distance from the well two girls were standing with their flock. On enquiring why they were there, the girls told Musa that their father was very old and there was no young man in their family to help them with their sheep. So they themselves came at the well to water their sheep. But they had

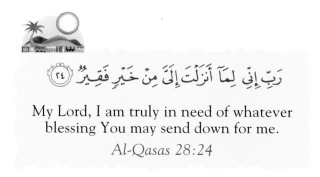

رَبِّ إِنِّي لِمَآ أَنزَلْتَ إِلَيَّ مِنْ خَيْرٍ فَقِيرٌ ﴿٢٤﴾

My Lord, I am truly in need of whatever
blessing You may send down for me.

Al-Qasas 28:24

110

to wait till other shepherds go home.

The Prophet Musa took pity on the two sisters. He led their sheep to the well and made them drink water. The girls were very happy. They took their sheep and went home.

Musa ﷺ Meets Shuayb ﷺ

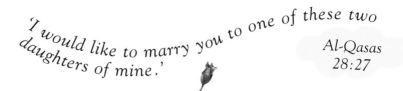

'I would like to marry you to one of these two daughters of mine.'

Al-Qasas
28:27

When the girls came home early, their father asked: "How come you are home so early!"

The sisters told their father that a young man helped them to water their sheep, so they did not have to wait.

The old man was the Prophet Shuayb ﷺ. He was sent by Allah to the people of Madyan to preach them about Allah. He immediately asked his daughters to bring Musa home. He told them he would pay him for his kind act.

Thus, the Prophet Musa came to the house of the Prophet

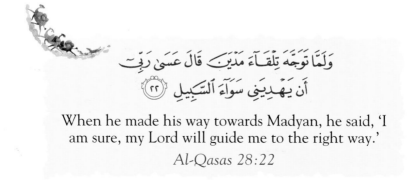

وَلَمَّا تَوَجَّهَ تِلْقَآءَ مَدْيَنَ قَالَ عَسَىٰ رَبِّيٓ
أَن يَهْدِيَنِي سَوَآءَ ٱلسَّبِيلِ ﴿٢٢﴾

When he made his way towards Madyan, he said, 'I
am sure, my Lord will guide me to the right way.'

Al-Qasas 28:22

Shuayb. He had food with the girls' father.
And he began to stay with the family. The
Prophet Shuayb employed Musa for tending
his flock. He married one of his daughters to
the Prophet Musa.

The Burning Brand

He noticed a fire in the direction of Mount Tur.

*Al-Qasas
28:29*

After living in Madyan for about ten years, the Prophet Musa decided to go back to Egypt. So he took his family and started to travel towards Egypt. They were crossing a valley in the mountains when the Prophet Musa saw a fire high on the mountainside.

He said: "Stay here. I can see a fire. I can bring you a brand from it, or find some guidance at the fire."

وَهُوَ ٱلَّذِى جَعَلَ لَكُمُ ٱلَّيۡلَ لِبَاسًا وَٱلنَّوۡمَ
سُبَاتًا وَجَعَلَ ٱلنَّهَارَ نُشُورًا ۝

It is He who made the night a mantle
for you, and sleep for repose; and made
the day a time for rising.

Al-Furqan 25:47

114

The Prophet Musa climbed the mountain. It was already dark. There was total silence. And then he heard a voice: "Musa, I am your Lord. I have chosen you. Listen to what I reveal to you. I am Allah. There is no god but Me. Serve Me. Remember Me and pray to Me."

The Divine Signs

Put your hand into your bosom; it will come out [shining] white.

Al-Qasas
28:32

After addressing Musa in the sacred valley of Tuwa, Allah ordered Musa: "Throw down your staff!"

So, when Musa ﷺ threw down his staff on the ground, it turned into a big snake! Then, Allah said, "Take hold of it, and have no fear."

Allah returned the staff to its former state. Allah gave the Prophet Musa another miracle. Allah asked him draw out his hand out of his armpit, and it was shining brightly, and then Allah said: "These are signs from Me."

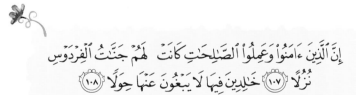

إِنَّ ٱلَّذِينَ ءَامَنُوا۟ وَعَمِلُوا۟ ٱلصَّٰلِحَٰتِ كَانَتْ لَهُمْ جَنَّٰتُ ٱلْفِرْدَوْسِ نُزُلًا ۝ خَٰلِدِينَ فِيهَا لَا يَبْغُونَ عَنْهَا حِوَلًا ۝

Those who believe and do good works shall
have the gardens of Paradise for their abode.
They shall forever dwell in the Gardens of
Paradise, desiring no change.

Al-Kahf 18:107-108

Then, Allah commanded Musa to go to Firawn and show him the signs and warn him, so that he might get guidance. Allah said to Musa, "Go to Firawn; he has transgressed all bounds."

The Prophet Musa asked Allah to send with him his brother the Prophet Harun who was an eloquent speaker. Musa said, "My brother Harun is more eloquent than I am. Send him with me to support me and back me up. For I fear that they will reject me."

The Prophet Harun ﷺ

Your request is granted, O Musa.

Ta Ha
20:90

When Allah commanded the Prophet Musa ﷺ to go to Firawn with His Signs and to tell him to stop doing cruelty on the Children of Israel, the Prophet Musa asked Allah to allow Harun to accompany him.

Harun ﷺ was Prophet Musa's brother, whom he loved and respected. Harun was noted for his beautifully refined way of speaking. He had escaped Firawn's order of killing the male child of the Children of Israel. Still, he was very careful of the Egyptians.

رَبَّنَا ٱكْشِفْ عَنَّا ٱلْعَذَابَ إِنَّا مُؤْمِنُونَ ﴿١٢﴾

Our Lord, relieve us from this torment,
for truly we are now believers in You.

Al-Dukhan 44:12

When Allah commanded the Prophet Musa to go to Firawn with Allah's Signs which He had given to the Prophet Musa and to warn him to stop spreading corruption and torturing the Children of Israel, Musa prayed to Allah to let Harun accompany him. "Your request is granted, O Musa," Allah said, and promised that he would now be safe.

The Prophet Harun accompanied the Prophet Musa to Firawn and they told him to believe in Allah and His message. But arrogant Firawn rejected Allah's message.

Musa ﷺ and the Magicians

For what they have wrought is only a magician's trick.

Taha 20:69

The Prophet Musa ﷺ went back to Egypt. He met Firawn and his ministers and told them to believe in Allah and obey Him. But Firawn refused to believe in Allah! He refused to bow down to Him. The Prophet Musa showed him the Signs of Allah but Firawn rejected these Signs and called his best magicians to fail Musa by their tricks. The magicians came and threw down their ropes and sticks and they looked like snakes of all sizes.

وَمَا تَنقِمُ مِنَّآ إِلَّآ أَنْ ءَامَنَّا بِـَٔايَـٰتِ رَبِّنَا لَمَّا جَآءَتْنَا رَبَّنَآ أَفْرِغْ عَلَيْنَا صَبْرًا وَتَوَفَّنَا مُسْلِمِينَ ﴿١٢٦﴾

You would punish us only because we believed in the signs of our Lord when they were shown to us. Our Lord, pour patience upon us, and cause us to die in a state of obedience to You.

Al-A'raf 7:126

120

Musa عليه السلام was horrified, as the snakes seemed to coil and uncoil around him. But Allah commanded Musa to throw down his staff. As Musa did so, all of a sudden, it became a huge snake and began to eat up all the other snakes one after another, until it had eaten them all up. Everyone was wonderstruck. The magicians fell on the ground in adoration, exclaiming, "We believe in the Lord of Musa and Harun!"

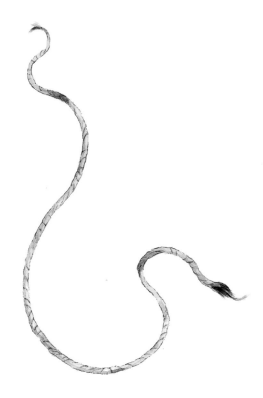

The Night Travellers

The Prophet Musa ﷺ was a Prophet of Allah and loved Allah. Allah loved him too, and every time there was a problem, the Prophet Musa asked Allah for help. Allah helped him and guided him.

He continued to preach in Egypt. But the torture of Firawn to the Children of Israel remained unabated. And when it became unbearable for the Children of Israel to bear, Allah asked Musa to leave Egypt. Allah said to Musa: "Travel by night with My servants, for you will surely be pursued." The Prophet Musa

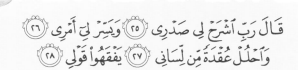

قَالَ رَبِّ ٱشۡرَحۡ لِي صَدۡرِي ﴿٢٥﴾ وَيَسِّرۡ لِيٓ أَمۡرِي ﴿٢٦﴾ وَٱحۡلُلۡ عُقۡدَةٗ مِّن لِّسَانِي ﴿٢٧﴾ يَفۡقَهُواْ قَوۡلِي ﴿٢٨﴾

He said, my Lord! open up my heart, and make my task easy for me. Loosen the knot in my tongue, so that they may understand my speech.

Ta Ha 20:25-28

called his people and told them to do exactly what Allah had said to him.

Accordingly, the Prophet Musa and his people left at night. There were many of them. And among them there were many women and children. The women and children walked very slowly and got tired very quickly. That is why the caravan did not move very fast. When Firawn learnt of it, he followed them with a huge army to capture and punish them.

The Sea Parted

Then We bade Musa strike the sea with his staff.

Al-Shu'ara'
26:52

After walking for some time, the Prophet Musa ﷺ and his people reached the shore of the sea.

Then they saw Firawn and his soldiers following them. They were moving very fast! They were on horses and soon they were to catch Musa and his people.

The Prophet Musa's people became frightened, for there was a huge sea on the front, they could not go anywhere! But Allah came to their help. Allah said to Musa: "Strike the sea with your stick!"

وَإِذَا سَأَلَكَ عِبَادِى عَنِّى فَإِنِّى قَرِيبٌ أُجِيبُ دَعْوَةَ ٱلدَّاعِ إِذَا دَعَانِ فَلْيَسْتَجِيبُوا۟ لِى وَلْيُؤْمِنُوا۟ بِى لَعَلَّهُمْ يَرْشُدُونَ ﴿١٨٦﴾

When My servants ask you about Me, say that I am near. I respond to the call of one who calls, whenever he calls to Me: let them, then, respond to Me, and believe in Me, so that they may be rightly guided.

Al-Baqarah 2:186

As soon as the stick touched the waves, a miracle happened! The sea parted! Allah made a path for them across the sea! Musa and his people hurried between the walls of water which were like mountains.

Firawn and his soldiers were right behind. But as soon as Musa and his people crossed the sea the passage closed and walls of the water collapsed. Firawn and his soldiers were drowned in the sea. None of them was saved. Allah is Mighty and Powerful. He helps those who love Him and pray to Him. He saves those who trust Him.

Manna and Salwa

Then We caused the clouds to provide shade for you and sent down for you manna and quails.

Al-Baqarah
2:57

After crossing the River of Nile, the Children of Israel breathed sighs of relief. They were very thankful to Allah for freeing them from Firawn's torture. They proceeded across the harsh Sinai desert in search of a new land in which to settle peacefully. After some time the food they had managed to carry ran out. They were tired and hungry.

But Allah provided them with food!

اَعۡدِلُوا هُوَ أَقۡرَبُ لِلتَّقۡوَىٰ وَاتَّقُوا اللَّهَ إِنَّ اللَّهَ خَبِيرٌ
بِمَا تَعۡمَلُونَ ۝ وَعَدَ اللَّهُ الَّذِينَ ءَامَنُوا وَعَمِلُوا
الصَّٰلِحَٰتِ لَهُم مَّغۡفِرَةٌ وَأَجۡرٌ عَظِيمٌ ۝

Deal justly; that is nearer to being God-fearing.
Fear God. God is aware of all that you do. God
has promised those who believe and do good deeds
forgiveness and a great reward.

Al-Ma'idah 5:8-9

Allah sent large flocks of quail from the sky which flew low over the tents of the Children of Israel. The birds rested on the ground near the tents of the Children of Israel, and it was very easy to catch them. The roasted quail meat was delicious.

Another amazing thing happened. When the people got up in the morning, they saw that the ground was covered with small round objects. These bits were a kind of white fresh dew, which the Prophet Musa's followers happily collected and ate. They tasted like sweet biscuits! They called it manna. In this way Allah saw that the Children of Israel obtained food without any exertion on their part.

The Twelve Springs

And there gushed out from it twelve springs.

Al-Baqarah
2:60

Allah bestowed on the children of Israel many blessings! The harsh sun made the desert burning hot. Allah again made a great favour to the Children of Israel. Allah made the clouds give them shade wherever they went.

As the days passed, the scarcity of water grew more severe. At Allah's command, Musa ﷺ struck a rock with his staff.

إِنَّمَا يُؤْمِنُ بِآيَاتِنَا الَّذِينَ إِذَا ذُكِّرُوا بِهَا خَرُّوا سُجَّدًا وَسَبَّحُوا بِحَمْدِ رَبِّهِمْ وَهُمْ لَا يَسْتَكْبِرُونَ ۩ ١٥ تَتَجَافَىٰ جُنُوبُهُمْ عَنِ الْمَضَاجِعِ يَدْعُونَ رَبَّهُمْ خَوْفًا وَطَمَعًا وَمِمَّا رَزَقْنَاهُمْ يُنفِقُونَ ١٦

The people who truly believe in Our messages are those who fall to the ground in prostration when they are reminded of them, and glorify their Lord with praise and are not arrogant. They forsake their beds, calling upon their Lord in fear and in hope, and spend out of what We have provided them with.

Al-Sajdah 32:15-16

Suddenly twelve springs gushed forth—one each for the twelve tribes of the Children of Israel.

The people drank their fill of the pure spring water and refreshed themselves.

Yet, after some time, instead of being grateful to Allah, the Children of Israel again began grumbling to Musa. They complained that they were "weary of eating one kind of food," and said to Musa: "Call on your Lord to give us some of the varied produce of the earth, green herbs and cucumbers, corn and lentils and onions."

Musa was astonished at their lack of gratitude. He worried about this tendency of his people to become selfish and greedy and forget about Allah, and he often went off by himself to pray to Allah for guidance to govern his people.

The Story of Cow

'O my people, you have indeed wronged your-
selves by worshipping the calf.' *Al-Baqarah*
2:60

The Children of Israel had started doubting a lot and kept themselves engaged in all sorts of unnecessary questioning on religious matters.

Once a wealthy man of the Children of Israel was murdered by his cousin, and the Children of Israel came to the Prophet Musa to find out the murderer. The Prophet Musa told them to sacrifice a heifer, as instructed by Allah. "Verily, Allah commands you that you slaughter a cow," told Musa ﷽.

But the Children of Israel did not believe Musa and started asking him to tell them all unnecessary details of the heifer in question. They said to Musa, "Call upon your Lord for us that He may make plain to us what it is!"

قَالَ رَبِّ إِنِّي ظَلَمْتُ نَفْسِي فَاغْفِرْ لِي

'Forgive me Lord, for I have sinned
against my soul.'
Al-Qasas 28:16

Musa said, "He says, 'Verily, it is a cow neither too old nor too young, but (it is) between the two conditions', so do what you are commanded."

But the Children of Israel persisted, "Call upon your Lord for us to make plain to us its colour."

Allah again revealed to the Prophet Musa who said to the Children of Israel: "He says, 'It is a yellow cow, bright in its colour, pleasing to the beholders.'"

But the Children of Israel persisted even more with asking about all other details, till they had exhausted with their questions. After this they sacrificed the heifer. But they were near to not doing the sacrifice, says Allah in the Quran. Allah did not like their questioning.

The story teaches us that believer should be eager to follow the command of Allah at the very first call. Such actions are liked by Allah and rewarded by Allah.

Appointed Nights

We appointed for Musa forty nights [on Mount Sinai].

Al-Baqarah
2:60

Allah had bestowed his grace on the Prophet Musa. One of the many favours of Allah given to him was that he used to talk with Allah. Because of this, the Prophet Musa is also known by the title of *Kalimullah*, the one who talked with Allah.

One day, Allah commanded the Prophet Musa to come on the mountain top for a communion with Him.

رَبَّنَا عَلَيْكَ تَوَكَّلْنَا وَإِلَيْكَ أَنَبْنَا وَإِلَيْكَ ٱلْمَصِيرُ ﴿٤﴾ رَبَّنَا لَا تَجْعَلْنَا فِتْنَةً لِّلَّذِينَ كَفَرُوا ۖ وَٱغْفِرْ لَنَا رَبَّنَا ۖ إِنَّكَ أَنتَ ٱلْعَزِيزُ ٱلْحَكِيمُ ﴿٥﴾

Our Lord, in You we have placed our trust and to You we turn in feeling sorry and to You is the final return. Our Lord, do not make us the victims of those who deny the truth, and forgive us our Lord. For You alone are the Mighty, the Wise One.

Al-Mumtahanah 60:4-5

When the Prophet Musa went on the appointed day on the Western side of the Mount Sinai, his heart was filled with love for Allah. He said to Allah: "My Lord! Show Yourself to me so that I may look at You!"

Allah said to Musa: "You cannot see Me, but look at the mountain; if it remains firmly in its place, then only will you see Me!"

The Prophet Musa looked at the far away mountain. When Allah's glory was manifested on the mountain, immediately the mountain crumbled away! Musa too fell down unconscious. When Musa came back to his senses, he cried to Allah: "Glory be to You!"

Allah Gives the Commandments

And We wrote for him upon the Tablets an admonition and details of all things.

Al-A'raf
7:145

At the communion with Allah for forty nights, the Prophet Musa was given by Allah tablets with commandments.

Allah said to the Prophet Musa, "Musa, I have chosen you of all mankind for My Messages and My Words. Hold fast to what I have given you, and be among the grateful!" These tablets contained the commandments for the Children of

وَإِن يَمْسَسْكَ ٱللَّهُ بِضُرٍّ فَلَا كَاشِفَ لَهُۥٓ إِلَّا هُوَۖ وَإِن يَمْسَسْكَ بِخَيْرٍ فَهُوَ عَلَىٰ كُلِّ شَىْءٍ قَدِيرٌ ۝ وَهُوَ ٱلْقَاهِرُ فَوْقَ عِبَادِهِۦۚ وَهُوَ ٱلْحَكِيمُ ٱلْخَبِيرُ ۝

If God should let any harm touch you, no one could
remove it except He; while if He should let some
good touch you, know that He has the power to do all
that He wills. He reigns Supreme over His servants;
and He is the All Wise, the All Aware.

Al-An'am 6:17-18

Israel to follow. "And We wrote for him upon the Tablets an admonition and details of all things, then [bade him]," Allah says in the Quran.

Then, Allah told the Prophet Musa, "Hold fast to them; and command your people to follow them in their best sense."

The commandments revealed to the Prophet Musa were in fact Torah. All believers have faith on the revelations sent to the Prophet Musa. The last revelation sent by Allah is the Quran which was revealed to the last Prophet of Allah, the Prophet Muhammad ﷺ.

The Trick of Samiri

*'We have tested your people in your absence.
The Samiri has led them astray.'*

Ta Ha
20:85

When Musa ﷺ returned from Mount Sinai after forty days, he was shocked and horrified by what he saw. There were the Children of Israel, dancing and shouting in drunken abandon around sacrificial fires, worshipping a golden calf! The Prophet Musa put the tablets aside and angrily addressed his people: "You sinned in my absence! Do you want Allah's punishment to reach you faster?"

The man responsible for this turned out to be Samiri (a Samaritan). He spread the rumour that Musa had abandoned

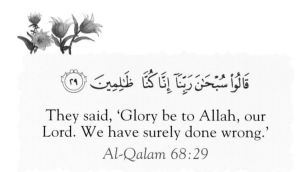

قَالُوا۟ سُبْحَٰنَ رَبِّنَآ إِنَّا كُنَّا ظَٰلِمِينَ ﴿٢٩﴾

They said, 'Glory be to Allah, our
Lord. We have surely done wrong.'

Al-Qalam 68:29

the Children of Israel, and then offered to provide them a new god. He collected their gold ornaments and melted them down into a calf.

Musa asked Samiri what had come over him, and then condemned him to live as an outcast. Samiri, as a result, lived like an outcast for the rest of his life saying "Touch me not!" to everyone he met. Then Musa burned the golden calf, and scattered its ashes over the sea. He admonished the Children of Israel and asked them to turn in repentance to Allah.

During the Absence of the Prophet Musa ﷿

'O My people! You are only being tested by this.'

Ta Ha
20:90

When the Prophet Musa ﷿ was leaving for Mount Sinai to spend thirty nights, he put his brother Harun ﷿ in charge of the Children of Israel. Musa told the Prophet Harun to be strong in holding these wayward people to the right path in his absence.

However, when Musa returned from Mount Sinai, he was shocked to see the Children of Israel worshipping a golden calf.

إِنَّ ٱللَّهَ فَالِقُ ٱلْحَبِّ وَٱلنَّوَىٰ يُخْرِجُ ٱلْحَيَّ مِنَ ٱلْمَيِّتِ وَمُخْرِجُ
ٱلْمَيِّتِ مِنَ ٱلْحَيِّ ذَٰلِكُمُ ٱللَّهُ فَأَنَّىٰ تُؤْفَكُونَ ﴿٩٥﴾

It is God who splits the seed and the fruit-stone.
He brings forth the living from the dead, and the
dead from the living. That is God. How then can
you, deluded, turn away from the truth?

Al-An'am 6:95

138

The Prophet Musa grabbed Harun by the hair and said: "Why didn't you come to find me when you saw this evil? Why did you disobey me?"

"Son of my mother," cried Harun, "The people overpowered me and almost did me to death. Do not let my enemies gloat over me; do not number me among the wrongdoers."

Harun explained to Musa hat he had told the people their Lord was only testing them and He would be Merciful. Harun asked them to follow his guidance. But they replied, "We will worship the golden calf until Musa returns."

The Story of Al-Khidr

And they found one of Our servants to whom We had granted Our mercy.

Al-Kahf
18:65

The Prophet Musa ﷺ set out with his young disciple, Yusha bin Nun to meet al-Khidr. At a certain point the fish they were carrying to eat revived and slipped away into the sea. Allah had told him, this is where they would find al-Khidr (probably an angel in the form of a man).

"May I follow you, so that you may guide me by what you have been taught?" Musa asked. Al-Khidr agreed but warned Musa to bear with him and not to question him about anything until he mentioned it himself. The two then embarked upon a ship, whereupon al-Khidr bored a hole in it.

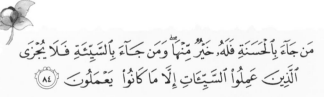

مَن جَآءَ بِٱلْحَسَنَةِ فَلَهُۥ خَيْرٌ مِّنْهَا ۖ وَمَن جَآءَ بِٱلسَّيِّئَةِ فَلَا يُجْزَى ٱلَّذِينَ عَمِلُوا۟ ٱلسَّيِّـَٔاتِ إِلَّا مَا كَانُوا۟ يَعْمَلُونَ ۝

He who does good shall be rewarded with something better. But he who does evil shall be requited according to his deeds.

Al-Qasas 28:84

Musa ﷺ exclaimed: "Have you made a whole in the boat to drown the people in it?"

"Didn't I tell you," replied al-Khidr, "that you would not bear with me patiently?"

"Forgive me," said Musa. They journeyed on until they met a young boy, whom al-Khidr promptly killed. Musa ﷺ exclaimed: "Indeed, you have done a terrible thing."

"Didn't I tell you," al-Khidr replied, "that you would not bear with me?" Musa ﷺ said: "If ever I question you again, abandon me."

Then they came to a city and asked for food, but were refused. Seeing a wall that was crumbling, al-Khidr repaired it, but Musa ﷺ objected to his doing so without payment. At this, Al-Khidr said, "Now we must part."

Al-Khidr Explains to Musa علیه السلام

But first I will tell you the meaning of the things you could not bear with patiently.

Al-Kahf
18:78

But before leaving, Al-Khidr explained to the Prophet Musa the reasons of his actions. Al-Khidr, the wise man, explained that he damaged the ship because it belonged to some poor fishermen and nearby there was a king who plundered every vessel.

As for the youth, he explained, he would only have distressed his believing parents with his wickedness and unbelief. We prayed that their Lord would replace him with a more righteous and filial son.

قُل لَّوْ كَانَ ٱلْبَحْرُ مِدَادًا لِّكَلِمَٰتِ رَبِّى لَنَفِدَ ٱلْبَحْرُ قَبْلَ أَن تَنفَدَ كَلِمَٰتُ رَبِّى وَلَوْ جِئْنَا بِمِثْلِهِۦ مَدَدًا ۝

Tell them, 'If the ocean became ink for writing the words of my Lord, surely the ocean would be exhausted before the words of my Lord came to an end—even if We were to add another ocean to it.'

Al-Kahf 18:109

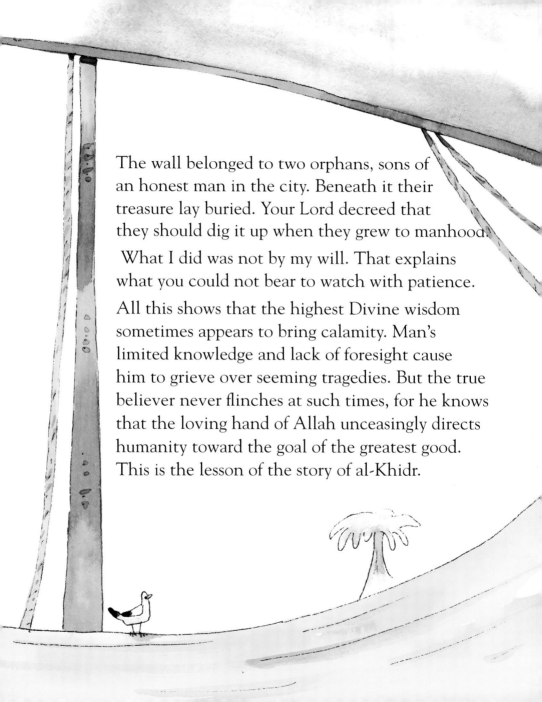

The wall belonged to two orphans, sons of an honest man in the city. Beneath it their treasure lay buried. Your Lord decreed that they should dig it up when they grew to manhood.

What I did was not by my will. That explains what you could not bear to watch with patience.

All this shows that the highest Divine wisdom sometimes appears to bring calamity. Man's limited knowledge and lack of foresight cause him to grieve over seeming tragedies. But the true believer never flinches at such times, for he knows that the loving hand of Allah unceasingly directs humanity toward the goal of the greatest good. This is the lesson of the story of al-Khidr.

The Ungrateful Qarun

'Do not exult in your riches, for God does not love the exultant.'

Al-Qasas
28:76

A man called Qarun or Korah lived in Egypt. He belonged to the children of Israel. Qarun had a huge treasure house full of gold and precious stones. The keys of the treasure house were huge and heavy.

People said to Qarun: "Do not exult in your riches, for Allah does not love the exultant. Be good to others as Allah has been good to you."

But, Qarun said proudly: "I have been given it only because of the knowledge I possess." Qarun did not fear Allah. He showed

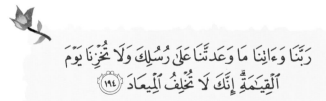

رَبَّنَا وَءَاتِنَا مَا وَعَدتَّنَا عَلَىٰ رُسُلِكَ وَلَا تُخْزِنَا يَوْمَ
ٱلْقِيَٰمَةِ إِنَّكَ لَا تُخْلِفُ ٱلْمِيعَادَ ﴿١٩٤﴾

Our Lord! Grant us what You have promised
to us through Your messengers, and do not
humiliate us on the Day of Resurrection.
Surely, You never fail to fulfil Your promise.

Al 'Imran 3:194

off his fine clothes, his jewels, and his palace. Some people were impressed with Qarun. But people who loved Allah said: "Allah's reward is better for those who believe and do good deeds."

Then a terrible thing happened! The earth opened up and swallowed Qarun! It swallowed Qarun, and his riches, and his treasure house together with its huge keys! The ungrateful and arrogant Qarun was dead with all his wealth!

The Prophet Shamuel علیه السلام

'They said, 'Appoint for us a king, and we will fight for the cause of God.'

Al-Baqarah
2:246

The Children of Israel once fell to vices and were totally disobedient to Allah. They committed many sins and killed whom they wished of the prophets. Then a tyrant king was sent by Allah who killed lots of them. They did not have prophet for a long time, then Allah sent Prophet, Shamuel علیه السلام, who taught them how to be good. He told them to leave vices and have fear of Allah. The Children of Israel asked Shamuel to appoint a king for them. They said to him: "Appoint for us a king and we will fight for the cause of God."

أَلَمۡ تَرَ إِلَىٰ رَبِّكَ كَيۡفَ مَدَّ ٱلظِّلَّ وَلَوۡ شَآءَ لَجَعَلَهُۥ
سَاكِنًا ثُمَّ جَعَلۡنَا ٱلشَّمۡسَ عَلَيۡهِ دَلِيلًا ﴿٤٥﴾

Have you not seen how your Lord lengthens
the shadows? Had He pleased, He could
have made them constant; then We placed
the sun as an indicator for them.

Al-Furqan 25:45

146

The Prophet Shamuel replied, "What if you refuse to fight, even if ordered to do so." They said, "Why should we not fight for the cause of God while we have been driven forth from our homes and our children?

Prophet Shamuel prayed to Allah for guidance. Allah revealed to him that He had chosen one, Talut, to be their king. Finally, the Prophet Shamuel told them that Allah had chosen Talut as their King.

The Pious Talut

Talut was a very pious, good and wise man. Shamuel led him to the Children of Israel and told them that Allah has appointed him as their king.

But the Children of Israel protested and said that how could Talut be their king when they were better in position and wealth than him.

The Prophet Shamuel told them: "God has chosen him over you, and has given him great knowledge and physique. God grants kingship to whoever He pleases: God is magnanimous and all knowing."

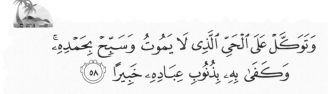

وَتَوَكَّلْ عَلَى ٱلْحَيِّ ٱلَّذِى لَا يَمُوتُ وَسَبِّحْ بِحَمْدِهِۦ وَكَفَىٰ بِهِۦ بِذُنُوبِ عِبَادِهِۦ خَبِيرًا ٥٨

Put your trust in the One who is the Ever-Living [God], who never dies, and glorify Him with His praise. He is fully aware of the sins of His servants.

Al-Furqan 25:58

But they insisted on a direct sign from Allah. At this Allah sent them signs. The Prophet Shamuel told them Allah will send to them the Ark of the Covenant with the relics of the Prophet Musa and the Prophet Harun and which will be carried by the angels. Finally, after seeing the Ark of the Covenant, the Children of Israel accepted Talut as their king.

The Army of King Talut

'God will test you with a river: whoever drinks from it is not with me.'

Al-Baqarah
2:249

After taking over as the King of the Children of Israel, The King Talut led an army to fight their enemy. His army reached a river and saw their enemies on the other bank waiting for them. Their army was even bigger than the army of King Talut! And a giant called Jalut was leading them!

The King Talut and his army were going to cross the river. Talut called his soldiers and said: "Allah will test you with a river: whoever drinks from it is not with me and whoever does not drink is with me."

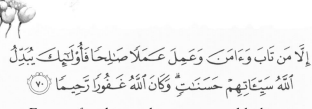

إِلَّا مَن تَابَ وَءَامَنَ وَعَمِلَ عَمَلًا صَٰلِحًا فَأُوْلَٰٓئِكَ يُبَدِّلُ ٱللَّهُ سَيِّـَٔاتِهِمْ حَسَنَٰتٍ ۗ وَكَانَ ٱللَّهُ غَفُورًا رَّحِيمًا ﴿٧٠﴾

Except for those who repent and believe
and do good deeds. God will change the evil
deeds of such people into good ones: He is
most forgiving and most merciful.

Al-Furqan 25:70

But the soldiers did not listen to their king. Almost all of them drank the river water. The King was left with only a few faithful soldiers.

But the army of their enemy was huge! The soldiers were very scared. They prayed to Allah: "Our Lord bestow patience upon us, make us stand firm, and help us against those who deny the truth."

The Prophet Dawud علیه السلام and the Giant Jalut

Dawud killed Jalut, and God gave him kingship and wisdom

Al-Baqarah
2:251

The Army of King Talut had a young man whose name was Dawud. He was a brave young man. Allah had bestowed him with great strength.

When Jalut came to fight, young Dawud came forward to fight against him. Everybody thought how young Dawud could match the strength of Jalut. But Allah was with Dawud. Allah had sent him to fight the enemy and save his people.

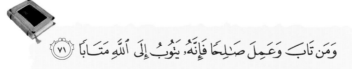

وَمَن تَابَ وَعَمِلَ صَٰلِحًا فَإِنَّهُۥ يَتُوبُ إِلَى ٱللَّهِ مَتَابًا ٧١

He who repents and does good deeds
has truly turned to God.

Al-Furqan 25:71

152

In a single shot of sling, Dawud killed the giant Jalut. And the small army of Talut defeated the army of their enemy.

Allah made Dawud a prophet and gave him a Book known as the Zabur, or the Psalm. Allah bestowed a great empire on him. The Prophet Dawud ruled in his kingdom with justice and equality. Allah had given him a beautiful voice and when he recited Psalm, birds also used to recite with him. Allah had made iron soft in his hand.

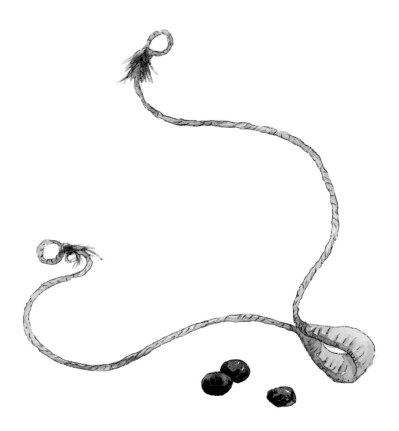

The Prophet Sulayman عليه السلام

Sulayman's hosts of jinn and men and birds, were all gathered together in his presence.

Al-Naml
27:17

The Prophet Dawud عليه السلام was given a big kingdom by Allah. He had a son whose name was Sulayman. He was also a prophet and ruled over a vast kingdom.

The Prophet Sulayman عليه السلام was a great king. He had a huge army. There were jinn, men and birds in his army. By the will of Allah, he commanded them all.

Allah taught the Prophet Sulayman the language of the birds. The Prophet Sulayman trained the birds. They worked in his army as messengers.

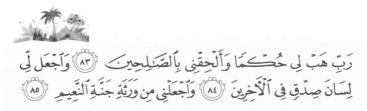

رَبِّ هَبْ لِى حُكْمًا وَأَلْحِقْنِى بِٱلصَّٰلِحِينَ ﴿٨٣﴾ وَٱجْعَل لِّى لِسَانَ صِدْقٍ فِى ٱلْءَاخِرِينَ ﴿٨٤﴾ وَٱجْعَلْنِى مِن وَرَثَةِ جَنَّةِ ٱلنَّعِيمِ ﴿٨٥﴾

My Lord, bestow wisdom upon me; unite me with the righteous; give me a good name among later generations; and make me one of those who will have a right to enter the Garden of Bliss.

Al-Shu'ara' 26:83-85

Allah loved Sulayman very much. Allah even gave him power to control wind. He was a just king and a true servant of Allah. Allah gave him wisdom too. The Prophet Sulayman also had many good horses and he loved them. But he never had vanity or pride. He did not flaunt his grandeur, but only for the sake of Allah.

Ants and the Prophet Sulayman عليه السلام

'Ants! Go into your dwellings, in case Sulayman and his hosts inadvertently crush you.'

Al-Naml
27:18

One day when the Prophet Sulayman ﷺ was marching across a valley with his army, he heard a voice. He looked around and saw a little ant speaking. The ant was calling to other ants: "O you ants run off home before Sulayman and his army treads on you by mistake!"

وَقَالَ رَبِّ أَوْزِعْنِيٓ أَنْ أَشْكُرَ نِعْمَتَكَ ٱلَّتِيٓ أَنْعَمْتَ
عَلَىَّ وَعَلَىٰ وَٰلِدَيَّ وَأَنْ أَعْمَلَ صَٰلِحًا تَرْضَىٰهُ
وَأَدْخِلْنِي بِرَحْمَتِكَ فِي عِبَادِكَ ٱلصَّٰلِحِينَ ﴿١٩﴾

'Lord, inspire me to be thankful for the blessings
You have granted me and my parents, and to do
good deeds that please You; and include me, by
Your grace, among Your righteous servants!'

Al-Naml 27:19

156

The Prophet Sulayman smiled. He knew the language of the birds. And he could also understand the language of the ants. He could understand the words of any creature on earth.

Then he was suddenly startled by the thought of how merciful Allah had been to him. He turned to his Lord in praise and thanked Him for His favour upon him. The Prophet Sulayman told his army to march carefully. He told them not to step on the ants.

The Queen of Saba

I found a woman ruling over them, who has been given everything.

Al-Naml
27:23

One day a bird, whose name was Hudhud, brought the news of the city of Saba to the Prophet Sulayman ﷺ. Hudhud told the Prophet Sulayman that the city was ruled by a Queen and all of them worshiped the sun instead of Allah.

The Prophet Sulayman wrote a letter to the Queen. "In the name of Allah, Most Gracious, Most Merciful. Don't be proud. Come to me in all submission."

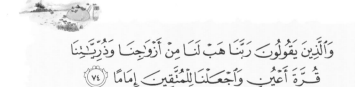

وَالَّذِينَ يَقُولُونَ رَبَّنَا هَبْ لَنَا مِنْ أَزْوَاجِنَا وَذُرِّيَّتِنَا قُرَّةَ أَعْيُنٍ وَاجْعَلْنَا لِلْمُتَّقِينَ إِمَامًا ﴿٧٤﴾

Who say, 'Lord, grant us joy in our wives and children and make us a model for the righteous.'
Al-Furqan 25:74

158

The Queen wanted to test the Prophet Sulayman first. She sent her ambassadors with many presents to him. But the Prophet Sulayman refused to accept her gifts. The Queen set out with her court to meet the Prophet Sulayman.

The Throne of the Queen

'O Counsellors, which of you can bring me her throne before they come to me in submission?'

Al-Naml
27:38

The Queen of Saba had a beautiful throne. When the Prophet Sulayman came to know that the Queen was coming to meet him, he wanted to have her throne brought at his palace, before she reached his palace.

The Prophet Sulayman asked his army of Jinn to bring it for him. One of Jinns named Ifrit brought the throne of the queen in a twinkling of an eye.

قَالَ رَبِّ ٱغْفِرْ لِي وَهَبْ لِي مُلْكًا لَّا يَنۢبَغِي
لِأَحَدٍ مِّنۢ بَعْدِيٓ إِنَّكَ أَنتَ ٱلْوَهَّابُ ﴿٣٥﴾

Lord forgive me! Grant me such power
as no one after me will have—You are
the Most Generous Provider.

Sad 38:35

When the Queen saw her throne she realised what power the Prophet Sulayman had. When she entered the palace she saw huge pool of water and picked her skirt so that her dress would not get wet. But the Prophet Sulayaman said to her that the palace was paved with glass.

The Queen realized she was taking unreal for real. She bowed her head and accepted Islam.

The Prophet Zakariyya ﷺ

Do not leave me heirless Lord, You are the best of heirs.'

Al-Anbiya'
21: 89

Long time ago, there lived in Jerusalem a prophet of Allah. His name was Zakariyya. Allah loved him, for he was pious. Men loved him because he was wise and just. Thus the Prophet Zakariyya ﷺ was loved both by Allah and by men.

Besides, the Prophet Zakariyya ﷺ was the high priest in the shrine of Jerusalem. He was a very respectable man on every count. At that time a little girl, Maryam or Mary, was given in

رَبِّ إِنِّي وَهَنَ ٱلْعَظْمُ مِنِّي وَٱشْتَعَلَ ٱلرَّأْسُ شَيْبًا وَلَمْ
أَكُنْ بِدُعَآئِكَ رَبِّ شَقِيًّا ۞

Lord, my bones have weakened and my head
has turned white with age, but never, Lord,
have I been disappointed in my prayer to you.

Maryam 19:4

service to Allah by her mother. She started to live in the shrine in Jerusalem.

As the Prophet Zakariyya ﷺ was her uncle, he became her guardian. He often visited Maryam in her little room. He noticed that she always had fresh food and fresh water.

The Prophet Zakariyya ﷺ was surprised and asked: "Maryam, from where do you get this food?" "It is from Allah," she answered, "Allah gives in plenty to anyone He wishes."

The Birth of the Prophet Yahya

'God gives you the good news of Yahya, who shall confirm the Word from God.'

Al 'Imran
3:39

The Prophet Zakariyya grew old and did not have any son. He was concerned for his kinsmen who were going wrong. He wanted a successor, a son, who could continue teaching his kinsmen about Allah.

He prayed to Allah: "Grant me a successor to be my heir and to be the heir of the House of Yaqub. And make him, O my Lord, acceptable to you".

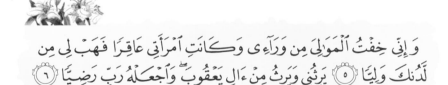

وَإِنِّي خِفْتُ ٱلْمَوَٰلِيَ مِن وَرَآءِى وَكَانَتِ ٱمْرَأَتِي عَاقِرًا فَهَبْ لِي مِن لَّدُنكَ وَلِيًّا ۝ يَرِثُنِي وَيَرِثُ مِنْ ءَالِ يَعْقُوبَ ۖ وَٱجْعَلْهُ رَبِّ رَضِيًّا ۝

Now I fear my kinsmen when I am gone. [I have no hope of their continuing my mission] for my wife is barren, so grant me a successor from Yourself, to be my heir and to be the heir [of the blessings] of the House of Yaqub; and make him, O my Lord, acceptable to you.

Maryam 19:5-6

164

Allah heard his prayer and said: "Zakariyya! We bring you good news of a son, whose name will be Yahya."

The Prophet Zakariyya ﷺ could not believe his luck. He said to Allah: "Give me a sign." Allah told him that he would not be able to speak to anyone for three successive days and night, although sound in body.

The Prophet Zakariyya ﷺ was very happy. He came out of the shrine. He could not speak but, through signs, he told people to pray to Allah. Thus, a son was born to old Zakariyya, he was named Yahya. Allah loved Yahya. He gave Yahya wisdom and made him His prophet.

The Most Honourable Woman

He has selected you over [all] the women.

Al 'Imran
3:42

Long, long ago there lived a pious lady called Hannah in Jerusalem. She prayed to Allah for a child and vowed that the child would spend his life serving Allah.

When she gave birth, it was a girl-child. She said, "O my Lord! I have given birth to a female."

Allah graciously accepted the girl-child and caused her to grow up in purity. She was named Maryam by her parents. When

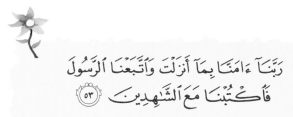

رَبَّنَآ ءَامَنَّا بِمَآ أَنزَلْتَ وَٱتَّبَعْنَا ٱلرَّسُولَ فَٱكْتُبْنَا مَعَ ٱلشَّٰهِدِينَ ۝

Our Lord, we believe in what You have sent down and we follow the Messenger, so count us among those who bear witness.

Al-'Imran 3:53

Maryam grew up she began serving Allah, as promised by her mother. The priests admired her deep devotion and love and respect for Allah. Everyone wanted to be her guardian. They drew lots and each time, it was in the favour of her uncle, the Prophet Zakariyya ﷺ. Thus Allah made the Prophet Zakariyya ﷺ her guardian. The Prophet Zakariyya ﷺ was an old man and he used to visit Maryam in her prayer niche. Maryam would spend most of her time in prayer and devotion. And soon, she became known for being good and pure. Allah says in the Quran, "We have set her above all other woman."

The Holy Son

'O Maryam, your Lord gives you good news of a Word from Him.'

Al 'Imran
3:39

One day Maryam was in her room praying. Suddenly an unknown man, who was actually an angel, appeared before her. She became afraid.

She said, "I seek refuge in the compassionate God from you; (do not come near me if you fear the Lord)."

But the man said: "Do not be afraid. I am Allah's messenger. You will have a holy son." Maryam was not married. She panicked. She asked the angel: "How can I have a son?"

The angel said: "God creates what He wills: when He wills a thing He need only say, "Be", and it is."

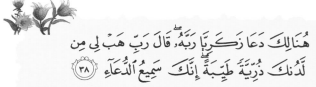

هُنَالِكَ دَعَا زَكَرِيَّا رَبَّهُۥ قَالَ رَبِّ هَبْ لِى مِن
لَّدُنكَ ذُرِّيَّةً طَيِّبَةً إِنَّكَ سَمِيعُ ٱلدُّعَآءِ ﴿٣٨﴾

Thereupon Zakariyya prayed to his Lord, saying,
'Lord, grant me by Your own grace virtuous
children. You are the hearer of all prayers.'

Al-'Imran 3:38

The angel also told her that the child's name would be Isa ibn Maryam and he would be honoured in this world and in the next, and that he would be among those who were granted nearness to God. He would be a Sign from Allah.

The angel also said: "O Maryam, God has selected you over all women of your time. O Maryam! Remain, truly devout to your Sustainer, and prostrate yourself in worship, and bow down with those who bow down before Him".

Isa ﷺ Speaks at Birth

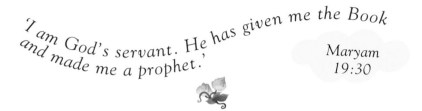

'I am God's servant. He has given me the Book and made me a prophet.'

Maryam
19:30

When the time for the birth of her child came, Maryam left Jerusalem. She walked till she reached a faraway place. She was tired and hot. She saw a palm tree. She sat in its shade. A stream was flowing nearby.

It was here, in the shade of a date palm and next to a stream, that the Prophet Isa (Jesus) ﷺ was born. Maryam heard a voice: "Do not despair. Your Lord has provided a brook that runs at your feet, and if you shake the trunk of this palm tree, it will drop fresh ripe dates on you."

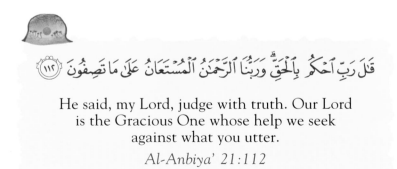

قَلَ رَبِّ ٱحْكُم بِٱلْحَقِّ وَرَبُّنَا ٱلرَّحْمَٰنُ ٱلْمُسْتَعَانُ عَلَىٰ مَا تَصِفُونَ ﴿١١٢﴾

He said, my Lord, judge with truth. Our Lord
is the Gracious One whose help we seek
against what you utter.

Al-Anbiya' 21:112

After the birth, Maryam picked up little Isa and went to her own village. People asked her: "Whose baby is this?" But she kept silent as Allah told her to.

Suddenly little Isa started speaking and the people were speechless. The little Isa said that he was a prophet of Allah and Allah had sent him with Injeel. But, still many people did not believe in the Prophet Isa.

The Prophet Isa علیه السلام
and his Miracles

And by God's leave I will heal the blind and the leper and bring the dead to life.

Al 'Imran 3:49

Allah gave the Prophet Isa power to perform miracles. So, when he grew up, he performed many miracles. He made little birds of clay and made them fly like real birds. He made a blind man see again. He restored a dead man to life.

It was Allah who helped the Prophet Isa to perform all these miracles. Allah loved him and looked after him.

ٱلْحَمْدُ لِلَّهِ ٱلَّذِى خَلَقَ ٱلسَّمَٰوَٰتِ
وَٱلْأَرْضَ وَجَعَلَ ٱلظُّلُمَٰتِ وَٱلنُّورَ

Praise be to Allah, who has created
the heavens and the earth and brought
into being darkness and light.

Al-An'am 6:1

The Prophet Isa had many disciples. They went everywhere with the Prophet Isa. They travelled from village to village and from town to town.

The Quran says: "Such was Isa, son of Maryam." He was a great prophet and he taught people how to love Allah.

Food from Heaven

'Can your Lord send down to us from heaven a table spread with food?'

Al-Ma'idah
5:112

One day the Prophet Isa ﷺ was travelling with his disciples to teach people about Allah. It was already evening. They were tired and sat in the field. They were also hungry. But they had no food with them.

One of the disciples said to the Prophet Isa: "Isa, son of Maryam. Can your Lord send down to us from heaven a table spread with food?"

قَالَ عِيسَى ٱبْنُ مَرْيَمَ ٱللَّهُمَّ رَبَّنَآ أَنزِلْ عَلَيْنَا مَآئِدَةً مِّنَ ٱلسَّمَآءِ تَكُونُ لَنَا
عِيدًا لِّأَوَّلِنَا وَءَاخِرِنَا وَءَايَةً مِّنكَ وَٱرْزُقْنَا وَأَنتَ خَيْرُ ٱلرَّٰزِقِينَ ١١٤

Isa ibn Maryam prayed, "Allah, our Lord! Send down
for us a table spread with food from heaven, so that it
may be a feast for us, for the first of us and for the last
of us: a sign from You. Give us what we need to live,
for You are the best of supporters."

Al-Ma'idah 5:114

The Prophet Isa did not like his words. He said to him: "Fear Allah, if you are a true believer." But the disciples ignored his words. They insisted: "We want to eat some food sent from heaven by Allah."

The Prophet Isa said to Allah: "Send down to us from heaven a table spread with food, that shall be for us a festival, the first and last of us, and a sign from You. And provide for us. You are the Best Provider."

Allah said: "I am sending you a table spread with food. But I will punish you if you do not believe Me after this. I will punish you more than any man has been punished ever before."

Allah Raised Isa علیه السلام to Himself

Allah said, 'O Isa, I shall take you to Me and will raise you up to Me.'

Al Imran
3: 55

Isa علیه السلام was a Prophet of Allah. He taught people how to love Allah. Allah bestowed him with power to perform any miracles.

Allah says in the Quran He instructed the Prophet Isa in the Book and in wisdom and in the Torah and in the Gospel.

The Prophet Isa continued his mission for several years, but only a few answered his call.

رَبِّ نَجِّنِي وَأَهْلِي مِمَّا يَعْمَلُونَ ﴿١٦٩﴾

My Lord, save me and my
family from their evil doings.

Al-Shu'ara' 26:169

176

Only some people saw the signs of Allah. There were some wicked people who disliked the Prophet Isa so much that they wanted to kill him.

The Children of Israel tried to crucify the Prophet Isa. But Allah saved him and they crucified another man, who was made to appear like him. Allah raised the Prophet Isa or Jesus in the heaven.

Dhul Qarnayn

We established him in the land, and gave him the means to achieve all things.

Al-Kahf
18:84

A long time ago, there lived a king called Dhul Qarnayn. Allah gave him a very vast kingdom. He ruled his kingdom very well. People loved him and obeyed him.

Dhul Qarnayn hated injustice. He hated it when some people treated other people badly. He was a just ruler. He treated all people fair.

قُلِ ٱللَّهُمَّ مَلِكَ ٱلْمُلْكِ تُؤْتِي ٱلْمُلْكَ مَن تَشَآءُ وَتَنزِعُ ٱلْمُلْكَ مِمَّن تَشَآءُ وَتُعِزُّ مَن تَشَآءُ وَتُذِلُّ مَن تَشَآءُ ۖ بِيَدِكَ ٱلْخَيْرُ ۖ إِنَّكَ عَلَىٰ كُلِّ شَىْءٍ قَدِيرٌ ﴿٢٦﴾

Say, O Lord, King of Kings. You give rulership to whom you will and take it away from whom You please; You raise up whoever You will and cast down whoever You will. All that is good lies in Your hands. You have the power to will anything.

Al 'Imran 3:26

178

All the time he travelled from one end of the kingdom to the other. He punished wicked people and rewarded the good ones.

Even after conquering a major part of the then inhabited world, Dhul Qarnayn had lost none of his humility. He gave the entire credit for his feats to the blessing of Allah.

The Iron Wall

One day Dhul Qarnayn reached the mountains. The people of the mountains came to him. They said: "O Dhul Qarnayn! Yajuj and Majuj (or Gog and Magog) are causing corruption on land... Set a barrier between us and them."

Dhul Qarnayn said: "Help me with a force of labourers and I will erect a barrier between you and them."

Dhul Qarnayn asked them to bring blocks of Iron. Then he filled the gap between the mountain sides with these iron

وَقُل رَّبِّ أَدْخِلْنِي مُدْخَلَ صِدْقٍ وَأَخْرِجْنِي مُخْرَجَ صِدْقٍ وَاجْعَل لِّي مِن لَّدُنكَ سُلْطَٰنًا نَّصِيرًا ﴿٨٠﴾

Say, my Lord, grant me an honourable
entrance and an honourable exit, and
sustain me with Your power.

Al-Isra' 17:80

180

blocks. He then asked them to heat the iron blocks, and when they were red with heat, Dhul Qarnayn poured molten brass on them. Thus the Iron Wall raised.

The Iron Wall closed the gap between the mountains. The people of Yajuj and Majuj, never troubled the mountain people again. After building the Iron Wall, Dhul Qarnayn said: "This is a blessing from my Lord. But when my Lord's promise has been fulfilled, He will level it to dust. And the promise of my Lord is true."

The People of the Cave

Do you think that the Men of the Cave and the Inscription were one of Our wondrous signs?

Al-Kahf
18:95

It happened a long, long time ago. The followers of the Prophet Isa (Jesus) ﷺ spread his teachings far and wide. They told people to believe in one God, follow the teaching of the Prophet Isa who was a prophet of Allah.

The king of the Roman Empire called Decius (Daqyanus) did not believe in the One God. He was against anyone who believed in God. He tried to put the followers of the Prophet Isa in jail.

رَبُّنَا رَبُّ ٱلسَّمَٰوَٰتِ وَٱلۡأَرۡضِ لَن نَّدۡعُوَاْ مِن
دُونِهِۦٓ إِلَٰهٗاۖ لَّقَدۡ قُلۡنَآ إِذٗا شَطَطًا ﴿١٤﴾

Our Lord is the Lord of the heavens and the earth.
Never shall we call upon any deity other than Him:
for that would be the worst thing we could do.

Al-Kahf 18:14

The beautiful city of Ephesus in Turkey was a part of the Roman Empire. Many people of Ephesus heard of the Prophet Isa. Among them were seven young men of noble families. They heard what the Prophet Isa's followers said about the One God. Allah guided them and they became true believers.

The king came to know about the seven young men. He sent his soldiers to capture them. But Allah saved them.

A Deep Sleep

Then We caused them to fall into a deep sleep for many years inside the cave.

Al-Kahf
18:11

To save themselves from the persecution by the King Decius, the seven men who were spreading the teachings of the prophet Isa ran for their lives.

They prayed to Allah: "O Lord! Show us Your Mercy and give us right guidance in our affair!" Suddenly they saw a cave in the forest. They were very tired. They lay on the ground in the cave to rest. Soon they fell asleep.

Allah kept them asleep for some three hundred years. They did not wake even once. They did not drink. They did not

فَقَالُوا۟ رَبَّنَآ ءَاتِنَا مِن لَّدُنكَ رَحْمَةً وَهَيِّئْ لَنَا مِنْ أَمْرِنَا رَشَدًا ۝

They said, 'Our Lord, grant us Your special mercy and give us right guidance in our affair.'

Al-Kahf 18:10

184

eat. And they did not make any sound. Only sometimes they turned on their sides. Their dog slept too, stretching his legs across the entrance to the cave.

The cave was in a deep forest. Its entrance was always in shade. Most people did not even notice it. And the few, who noticed it, were frightened off by the darkness. The sleeping men were completely safe. Allah saved them.

Luqman the Wise

We bestowed wisdom on Luqman.

Luqman
31:12

A long time ago, there lived a very, very wise man. His name was Luqman. He was wise, because Allah made him wise. Allah gave him wisdom and asked him to be thankful to the Almighty.

One day Luqman called his son. He gave him good many pieces of advice. This is what he said to him: "My son, do not associate anything with Allah. Associating others with Him is a terrible wrong."

رَبَّنَآ ءَاتِنَا فِى ٱلدُّنْيَا حَسَنَةً وَفِى ٱلْأَخِرَةِ
حَسَنَةً وَقِنَا عَذَابَ ٱلنَّارِ ﴿٢٠١﴾

Our Lord, grant us good in this world as well as good in the world to come, and protect us from the punishment of the Fire.

Al-Baqarah 2:201

Luqman also told his sons that Allah sees everything. He hears everything. He can see, even if something is hidden. Luqman said, "O my son! Though it be but the weight of a grain of mustard seed and though it be hidden in a rock, or in the heavens or on the earth, God will bring it forth. Truly, God is the knower of all subtleties and He is aware."

Luqman's Advice
to His Son

[We said] Give thanks to Me and to your parents; all will return to Me.

Luqman
31:14

Luqman gave his son some more advice. What beautiful advice! We all must listen to Luqman's advice.

He advised his son: "O my dear son! Say your prayers regularly, and enjoin good, and forbid evil, and endure patiently whatever may befall you."

وَلَوْ أَنَّمَا فِى ٱلْأَرْضِ مِن شَجَرَةٍ أَقْلَـٰمٌ وَٱلْبَحْرُ يَمُدُّهُۥ مِنۢ بَعْدِهِۦ سَبْعَةُ أَبْحُرٍ مَّا نَفِدَتْ كَلِمَـٰتُ ٱللَّهِ إِنَّ ٱللَّهَ عَزِيزٌ حَكِيمٌ ۝

If all the trees on earth were pens, and the sea were ink, with seven more seas added to it, the words of Allah would not be exhausted: for, truly, Allah is Almighty and Wise.

Luqman 31:27

Luqman further advised, "Do not avert your face from people out of haughtiness and do not walk with pride on the earth: for, behold, God does not love arrogant and boastful people."

"Walk modestly and lower your voice, for the ugliest of all voices is the braying of the ass."

The Prophet Uzayr ﷺ and His Donkey

God caused him to die, and after a hundred years, brought him back to life.

Al-Baqarah
2:259

The Prophet Uzayr, or Ezra ﷺ, was a pious man. He had a donkey on which he used to travel far and wide.

Once he was passing through a lonely city. The houses were all in ruins and no one lived there. "How will Allah restore it to life after its destruction," wondered Uzayr. There and then Allah caused him and his donkey to die. Allah brought the Prophet Uzayr back to life after 100 years!

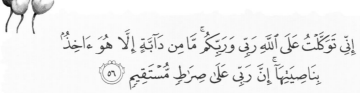

إِنِّي تَوَكَّلْتُ عَلَى ٱللَّهِ رَبِّي وَرَبِّكُم مَّا مِن دَآبَّةٍ إِلَّا هُوَ ءَاخِذٌ بِنَاصِيَتِهَآ إِنَّ رَبِّي عَلَى صِرَٰطٍ مُّسْتَقِيمٍ ﴿٥٦﴾

I have put my trust in Allah, my Lord and your Lord. For there is no living creature which He does not hold by its forelock. My Lord is on the straight path.

Hud 11:56

But the donkey on which he had been travelling was reduced to bones. Allah reunited the bones, clothed them with flesh and gave life to the donkey. "How long have you remained in this state?" asked Allah.

"A day or part of a day," replied a puzzled Uzayr.

"No," said Allah, "You have remained in this state for a hundred years."

But Uzayr was amazed to see that his food and drink was intact and fresh. Seeing all this happening in front of his own eyes, the Prophet Uzayr was struck dumb and exclaimed: "Now I know that Allah has power over all things."

The story is told to reaffirm belief in the Hereafter and life after death.

The Story of Two Gardens

Recite to them the parable of two men! One of them We provided with two vineyards.

Al-Kahf
18:32

A long, long ago, there lived two friends, one a rich gardener, and the other a poor farmer. One day the gardener showed the poor farmer around his garden and proudly said to him, "I am richer than you and have a bigger following! And I do not think this will ever perish! And I do not believe that the hour of Doom will ever come."

When the poor farmer saw his friend behave in this wicked way, he asked: "Do you deny Him who created you from dust, from a small drop of liquid, and fashioned you into a man?

وَهُوَ ٱلَّذِى يُنَزِّلُ ٱلْغَيْثَ مِنْ بَعْدِ مَا قَنَطُوا۟ وَيَنشُرُ
رَحْمَتَهُۥ وَهُوَ ٱلْوَلِىُّ ٱلْحَمِيدُ ٢٨

It is He who sends rain after they have lost hope
and spreads His mercy far and wide.
He is the Protector, Worthy of All Praise.

Al-Shura 42:28

As for myself, Allah is my Lord, and I will associate no one else with Him."

"Instead of entering the garden proudly, you should have acted humbly and glorified Allah."

The very next day the rich man's garden was laid waste. He looked at his ruined garden. Realizing his mistake, he cried that he should not have been proud. He said, "Would that I had not associated anyone with my Lord."

He turned to Allah for help. It was too late to save his garden, but not too late to save his soul. This story is meant to teach believers never to speak proudly of himself or of his riches.

Love your Parents

And treat them (parents) with humility and tenderness.

Al-Isra'
17:24

Numerous passages in the Quran and sayings of the Prophet Muhammad ﷺ enjoin the believer to be good and courteous to his parents. This duty is an even greater necessity when the parents enter upon old age.

Thus the Quran reminds us: "And be kind to your parents. If one or both of them attain old age with you, do not utter a word of contempt and show them no sign of impatience but

وَقَضَىٰ رَبُّكَ أَلَّا تَعْبُدُوٓا۟ إِلَّآ إِيَّاهُ وَبِٱلْوَٰلِدَيْنِ إِحْسَٰنًا ۚ إِمَّا يَبْلُغَنَّ عِندَكَ ٱلْكِبَرَ أَحَدُهُمَآ أَوْ كِلَاهُمَا فَلَا تَقُل لَّهُمَآ أُفٍّ وَلَا تَنْهَرْهُمَا وَقُل لَّهُمَا قَوْلًا كَرِيمًا ﴿٢٣﴾

Your Lord has commanded that you should worship none but Him, and show kindness to your parents. If either or both of them attain old age with you, say no word of contempt to them and do not rebuke them, but always speak gently to them

Al-Isra' 17:23

194

speak to them kind words. Treat them with humility and tenderness…"

The Quran urges us to pray for our parents: "Lord, bestow Your mercy on them, as they raised me up when I was little."

We are reminded of our parents' painstaking care in our upbringing, especially that of our mother. The Quran says: "We enjoined man to show kindness to his parents, for with much pain his mother bears him, and he is not weaned before he is two years of age." After his duty towards his Lord, the first duty of an individual is towards his parents.

The Believers in Paradise

Those who believe and do good works shall have the gardens of Paradise for their abode.

Al-Kahf
18:107

Believers are promised by Allah that they will be given Paradise in the life after death. It shall be the greatest gift from Allah for their good actions and their bowing to the will of Allah at all times.

On the Last Day there here shall be no idle talk, no lies, no sinful speech—only the greeting, "Peace! Peace!"

The believers shall rest on jewelled couches and carpets richly spread. Trees will spread their shade around them, and fruits such as dates and pomegranates will hang in bunch over them.

رَبَّنَا إِنَّكَ تَعْلَمُ مَا نُخْفِي وَمَا نُعْلِنُ وَمَا يَخْفَىٰ عَلَى ٱللَّهِ
مِن شَىْءٍ فِى ٱلْأَرْضِ وَلَا فِى ٱلسَّمَآءِ ﴿٣٨﴾

Our Lord, You have knowledge of all that we hide
and all that we reveal: nothing in heaven or on
earth is hidden from Allah.

Ibrahim 14:38

Rivers will flow through the gardens, the fruits of which will all be within their reach.

Allah will give believers pure nectar to drink. There shall flow rivers of the purest water, and rivers of the clearest honey, rivers of milk forever fresh, and rivers of wine tasting sweet to those who drink it. (Such wine will neither hurt their heads nor take away their reason).

But the most blessed thing to happen in Paradise will be meeting with the Lord Himself. And the Lord will say to his good righteous servants: "O soul at peace! Return to your Lord, joyful, and pleasing in His sight. Join My servants and enter My Paradise."

The Quran was Revealed

Read! In the name of your Lord, who created: created man from a clot [of blood].

Al-'Alaq
96:1-2

The Prophet Muhammad ﷺ would often sit alone in the cave of Hira, near Makkah. He would pray and meditate there, surrounded by nature.

One night during Ramadan, the Prophet sat all alone as usual in the cave. Suddenly the angel Jibril (Gabriel) appeared before him in human form and taught him the very first verses of the Quran. The Prophet felt they were actually being written on

ٱلْحَمْدُ لِلَّهِ ٱلَّذِى هَدَىٰنَا لِهَٰذَا وَمَا كُنَّا لِنَهْتَدِىَ لَوْلَآ
أَنْ هَدَىٰنَا ٱللَّهُ لَقَدْ جَآءَتْ رُسُلُ رَبِّنَا بِٱلْحَقِّ

All praise belongs to Allah who has guided
us to this. Had Allah not guided us, we would
never have found the way. The messengers of
our Lord brought the Truth.

Al-A'raf 7:43

his heart. The Quran thus began to be revealed by Allah to the Prophet Muhammad ﷺ.

All this took 23 long years to complete. The Prophet began giving the message of the Quran to the people of Makkah, as ordered by Allah. But not many of them liked his teachings and they became his dire enemies. They all set out to harm him and his handful of followers.

Al-Isrā and Al-Mirāj

Holy is He who took His servant by night from the sacred place of worship to the remote house of worship.

Al-Isra'
17:1

When the Makkan persecution of the Prophet and his family seemed about to crush Islam, the Prophet Muhammad ﷺ had an extraordinary experience, known as al-Isra and al-Miraj, or the Night Journey and the Ascension.

One night, as he slept next to the Kabah, the Archangel Jibril woke him and took him on a strange, white winged animal, called Buraq, from Makkah to al-Aqsa mosque in faraway Jerusalem. From there Jibril took the Prophet through

سُبْحَٰنَ ٱلَّذِىٓ أَسْرَىٰ بِعَبْدِهِۦ لَيْلًا مِّنَ ٱلْمَسْجِدِ ٱلْحَرَامِ إِلَى ٱلْمَسْجِدِ ٱلْأَقْصَا ٱلَّذِى بَٰرَكْنَا حَوْلَهُۥ لِنُرِيَهُۥ مِنْ ءَايَٰتِنَآ إِنَّهُۥ هُوَ ٱلسَّمِيعُ ٱلْبَصِيرُ ۝

Holy is He who took His servant by night from the sacred place of worship [at Makkah] to the remote house of worship [at Jerusalem]—the precincts of which We have blessed, so that We might show him some of Our signs. Surely, it is He who is All Hearing, and All Seeing.

Al-Isra' 17:1

Heaven's gates, where he saw countless angels. He was then taken through the Seven Heavens, one by one. Then, the Prophet passed through many veils, until at last he came into the divine Light of Allah's Presence, which brought peace and banished all sense of time. Then, he was brought back to earth where he was amazed to find the spot where he had lain still warm, and the cup he had tipped over still emptying. This had all taken place in less than a moment!

The next morning, the Prophet Muhammad 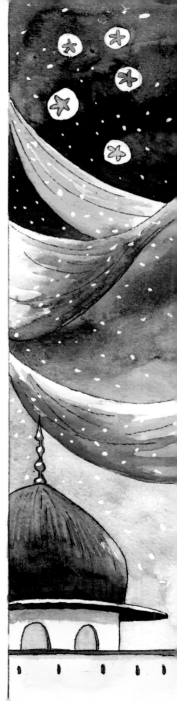 told the Quraysh of his experience. But many doubted his word. However, the Prophet's description of Jerusalem, and the caravans he had seen on his return to Makkah, convinced them of his truthfulness.

The Migration to Madinah

If you do not support him [Muhammad], know that God did support him.

Al-Tawbah
9:40

One night, at his Lord's command, the Prophet Muhammad ﷺ left Makkah for Madinah along with Abu Bakr. The Makkans were looking for him to kill him. So, to throw the attackers off the scent, they left Ali Ibn Ali Talib lying in the Prophet's bed. Once out of Makkah, they sheltered in the nearby cave of Thawr.

On their third day there, a search party approached the cave where they were hiding. Abu Bakr, the Prophet's companion

ادْعُ إِلَىٰ سَبِيلِ رَبِّكَ بِالْحِكْمَةِ وَالْمَوْعِظَةِ الْحَسَنَةِ وَجَادِلْهُم بِالَّتِي هِيَ أَحْسَنُ إِنَّ رَبَّكَ هُوَ أَعْلَمُ بِمَن ضَلَّ عَن سَبِيلِهِ وَهُوَ أَعْلَمُ بِالْمُهْتَدِينَ ﴿١٢٥﴾

Call to the way of your Lord with wisdom and fair exhortation
and reason with them in a way that is best. Your Lord knows
best those who have strayed away from His path, and He
knows best those who are rightly guided.

Al-Nahl 16:125

in this journey, became afraid. But the Prophet consoled Abu Bakr by saying that Allah was with them. Their pursuers soon went away after conducting their search.

No one had cared to look inside the cave. But it had been a close shave. Later, travelling only at night for safety, and taking a long winding route, they reached Madinah in seven days. They were joyously received and then were greatly helped by the Madinans to spread the message of Islam from family to family and from tribe to tribe and ultimately to all parts of the world.

The Treaty of Peace

Truly, We have granted you a clear victory.

Al-Fath
48:1

The Prophet Muhammad ﷺ once left for Makkah to perform Umrah accompanied by 1400 companions. He camped at Hudaybiyah, a short way from Makkah. It was a completely peaceful march. But the Makkan leaders objected to it.

They felt that their prestige was damaged by the fact that the very people who had been expelled by them from Makkah should come to the city again and perform the rights of Umrah openly and in such large numbers.

دَعۡوَىٰهُمۡ فِيهَا سُبۡحَـٰنَكَ ٱللَّهُمَّ وَتَحِيَّتُهُمۡ فِيهَا سَلَـٰمٌ وَءَاخِرُ دَعۡوَىٰهُمۡ أَنِ ٱلۡحَمۡدُ لِلَّهِ رَبِّ ٱلۡعَـٰلَمِينَ ﴿١٠﴾

They will call out 'Glory be to You, O Allah!', while their greeting in it will be: 'Peace!' And the close of their call will be, 'All praise is due to Allah, the Lord of the Universe!'

Yunus 10:10

Now the Prophet halted at Hudaybiyah and began negotiating for peace with the Makkan leaders. The Quraysh finally agreed to sign a peace treaty specifying that for the next ten years no war would take place between the Muslims and the Makkans.

By the terms of this treaty, the Muslims were to go back without visiting the Kabah. They were to come again the following year and stay in Makkah for just three days.

The companions of the Prophet were very upset at the terms of the treaty, it seemed to them that the Makkans had been dominant and they were made out to be subservient. But God declared in the Quran that it was a 'Clear Victory' for the believers. The future events showed how the Treaty of Hudaybiyah paved the way for the spread of Islam across Arabia.

The Message of Peace

We have sent you forth as a mercy to all mankind.

Al-Anbiya'
21:107

A great part of the Prophet's mission was to bring peace to the world. One way of doing so was to convince people that all men and women, although living in very different regions of the world, and seemingly different from one another in colour, culture and language, etc., were in fact each other's blood brothers and sisters. The Prophet would preach to his followers: "You are all Adam's offspring and Adam was made of clay." And in his prayers to his Creator, he would say, "O

وَقَالُوا۟ ٱلْحَمْدُ لِلَّهِ ٱلَّذِىٓ أَذْهَبَ عَنَّا ٱلْحَزَنَ إِنَّ رَبَّنَا لَغَفُورٌ شَكُورٌ ۝ ٱلَّذِىٓ أَحَلَّنَا دَارَ ٱلْمُقَامَةِ مِن فَضْلِهِۦ لَا يَمَسُّنَا فِيهَا نَصَبٌ وَلَا يَمَسُّنَا فِيهَا لُغُوبٌ ۝

Praise be to Allah who has taken away all sorrow from us. Our Lord is forgiving and understanding. Through His grace He has admitted us to the everlasting Abode, where neither toil nor weariness affects us.

Fatir 35:34-35

206

Lord, all your servants are brothers." The Prophet himself set an example of peaceful living with his great gentleness, kindness, humility, good humour and excellent common sense, and his great love for all people and even for animals. He never made others feel small, unwanted or embarrassed. He urged his followers to do likewise, to release slaves whenever possible, and give alms, especially to very poor people, orphans and prisoners—without any thought of reward. He would tell people that "every religion has some special virtue, that of Islam being modesty." Without such a virtue, no community can have lasting peace. He was of a high moral character, so that people might harm him, yet he would pray for them, returning good for evil. When others tried to provoke him, he would remain patient and serene. In setting this example, his real aim was to fashion souls which were turned towards God, which found Allah so great that everything else seemed unimportant.

Books for Little Hearts!

365 Days with the SAHABAH

QURAN KNOWLEDGE GAME
The world of the Quran in just one box

Awesome QURAN Questions and Answers

Arabic Alphabet

365 Dua with Stories
Everyday Stories Based on Prayers

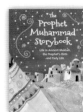
The Prophet Muhammad Storybook
Life in Ancient Makkah, the Prophet's Birth and Early Life

All About Akhlaaq

365 Hadith with Stories
Everyday Stories Based on the Sayings of the Prophet Muhammad

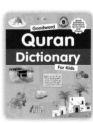
365 Days with the PROPHET MUHAMMAD

QURAN ACTIVITY BOOK For Kids

The Story of Khadija
The First Muslim and the Wife of the Prophet Muhammad

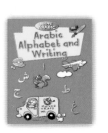
Goodword Quran Dictionary For Kids

The Prophet Muhammad Storybook
Marriage, Prophethood and Early Days in Makkah

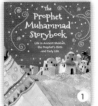
AWESOME QURAN FACTS
A colourful reference guide

Arabic Alphabet and Writing